"*Expose Yourself* turned out to be a page turner for me—I did not put the book down and read it in one day."

"Erin's stories about life as a stripper are fascinating and amusing in their own right, but those life lessons are exactly the ones I would choose for everyone to learn."

"I never would have connected stripping with learning some of the most important and profound life lessons in humanism and critical thinking, but Erin's *Expose Yourself* manages to do just that."

"Erin managed to humanize stripping in my view, and has passed along her learnings about giving it your all and daring to be yourself in a judgmental world."

"The overall message Erin conveys is to make damn sure you're living for and fighting for life on your own terms."

"Erin Louis provides an in-depth view of her work as a stripper and its impact on being a daughter, wife, colleague, friend and fellow sister. Her insights helped me rethink my life in every chapter!"

"What a unique concept! Advice from a former stripper? Don't mind if I do! Great life lessons, ideas and answers to your burning questions in this fun and lively book! I read it in one night!"

Readers may write to Erin at Erin@ErinLouis.com

Expose Yourself

How to Take Risks, Question Everything and Find Yourself

Humor and Insights From My Life as a Stripper

Erin Louis

To Amanda,
My fellow
Atheist mom
and friend,

— Louis

Contributing Editor and Cover Photos by Judy Saint

Cover Art by Joe Menendez

ISBN: 9781073690671

LCCN: 2019908373

PCN: 9781073690671

Independently published

This book is dedicated to all those who may
be still hiding from who they really are.

Table of Contents

Chapter 1

Take It From a Stripper

How Being a Stripper Taught Me to Take Risks, Stop Pretending, and Challenge Norms

You might be asking yourself, "What could a stripper possibly say that would relate to me?" In fact, I'd be terribly disappointed in you if you weren't asking that question. It's a perfectly valid one. After all, what does my twenty years of public nudity have to do with you? Well, now that you ask, quite a bit.

While common stereotypes often portray strippers as amoral, drug dependent, uneducated, and broken human beings, this is not always the case. A common misconception is that most strippers are driven to the profession out of desperation, a last resort, or simply lacking the cognitive ability to make it in the real world. I would say that description is much more fitting of today's reality TV stars than your average stripper. Actually, most strippers are smart, independent and happy to be on the fringe of society.

My time in the adult industry has given me a unique perspective on not only sex, but also on taking risks, questioning norms, thinking for myself, and so much more. I knew I would likely learn much about sex, but my job actually taught me so much more about life itself. How to ask unwelcome questions, how to accept other people, and how to let go of limiting thoughts and beliefs. I've essentially performed an informal sociological study on humans. Granted my knowledge is limited to the context of the strip club, but I've come up with some interesting findings, including, of course, how it relates to human sexual behavior. For example, sex shaming, especially from religions, seems to be the driving force behind the whole sex industry itself. I firmly believe that if sex and nudity were not deemed to be wrong or dirty, strip clubs, porn, and the like wouldn't exist at all. While I'd like to think I might qualify as a subject matter expert, I have no formal education in the field. My expertise comes strictly from twenty sober years working with strippers, strip club staff and customers. My advice and opinions all stem from that experience.

While I have made it out of the industry with my cognitive faculties mostly intact, I must admit I have a slightly twisted view on a few things. As most of us are taught to conceal our inner selves for fear of judgement, I see it mostly in the open. Thirty seconds in someone's lap for instance, can give me a wealth of information about that person. I can tell pretty quickly someone's feelings toward women and whether he calls his mother regularly or not. Things like fetishes, or the way someone talks or touches, are each a little clue into someone's mind. On the surface it seems like all I do is provide live masturbatory material, while in reality I'm collecting information. I have insights that can only come from my work, and that includes other dancers as well as staff. The way people interact in the strip club can be very different from the way they act in what I will refer to as the real world.

When you expose yourself both literally and figuratively, you are casting a light on reality. The lessons I learned in the strip club apply not only to other people but also to myself. I was forced to face certain things about myself that I may have missed had I taken a more mainstream path in life. Seeing yourself for who you really are on the inside is in my opinion the only way to true happiness. To be able to reach your goals, you must first be honest with yourself, and that includes everything that makes you uncomfortable. Whether suppressed feelings, desires, or insecurities, refusing to face uncomfortable truths about yourself and the reality you live in, is a terrific way to end up a bitter, unfulfilled and miserable person. Frankly, that sucks for not only you, but everyone else you come in contact with.

As a stripper, exposing my outside to public scrutiny also eventually led to exposing the uncomfortable feelings and doubts about the world around me and what I was taught to believe. Getting naked on stage forced me to come to terms with the inadequacies I felt I had physically. As I grew more comfortable confronting my fears about aesthetic judgements, I was able to turn that into acknowledging the uncomfortable feelings I was holding inside. Dancing showed me how to present a fantasy, which in turn gave me the tools to recognize when I myself was presented with a fantasy, as well as the fantasies I was presenting to myself.

I was taught that living a happy life meant living a normal one. Stay in your lane and go with the flow. Be what society considers acceptable and respectable. When I was finally able to let go of the image of what people thought I should be and started to investigate the world around me, what I found was far more profound and beautiful than anything I had ever thought it could be.

I hope to help you live your best life, learn to take risks, question everything, and find yourself. Also, I hope to show you that a life without risks is ultimately boring and unfulfilling. The good news is you don't have to get naked in public to do it, as I've very generously already done that for you.

Chapter 2

A Risky Proposition

The Value of Taking Risks, and the Danger of Not

Exposing myself as a stripper at age eighteen, I had no idea of the risks involved. I understood what society thought about the profession, so I knew I would likely be judged harshly. I also knew my family would have some reservations, maybe serious enough to affect my relationship with them. I had no adequate grasp, though, of the perils of trying to remain upright in six-inch stilettos combined with lotion smeared on the stage, or the physical risks to my body. Yet, I wasn't happy with the trajectory of my life at the time, and knew I wanted something different. So, I took a risk.

Every day we take risks. Just getting out of bed can be risky. After all, you could slip and fall on your way to the bathroom, or scratch your cornea putting in your contacts, or even have a heart attack straining on the toilet. On second thought, maybe you should just stay in bed. Think about it, almost everything you do has the potential to go sideways and kill you. People die or get severely injured every day doing mundane and seemingly harmless tasks. If everything is so risky, why do we even bother?

We bother because a life without risks would be no life at all, or at least boring, pointless, and completely without purpose. There is an episode of SpongeBob SquarePants that illustrates this point, in my opinion brilliantly. SpongeBob decides that he will be safer by staying indoors and never going outside. He ends up making friends with a potato chip and a used tissue, and eventually losing whatever is in his head that would constitute a mind. As silly as that is, the thong-wearing cartoon sponge has a good point. If you avoid all risks, you could end up talking to your own snot rag. So, go ahead and jump off a cliff. Really, go ahead, just make sure you're attached to a hang glider, bungee cord, or some other device designed to stop you from dying. It may not prevent you from soiling yourself, but statistically speaking, it should make sure you live to tell the story.

Getting Naked

The idea of becoming a stripper first occurred to me while perusing the want ads in the local paper. With the internet still in its infancy, the newspaper was the only way I knew to look for a job. I was working at a job which confined me to a poorly constructed cubicle answering phones, desperately trying to get the people who called in to buy something they didn't need. I was looking for really anything other than what I was currently doing. I wanted to be excited to go to work, or at the very least, I wanted to stop fantasizing about running my car into a tree. Not that I was suicidal, I just thought a few days in the hospital would be a nice change from the mind-numbing job I was working.

I ran across an ad for exotic dancers. This was an outcall service for dancers to do private shows, such as bachelor parties. The name of the business was called "Take It Off." My immediate thought was, "As in take off my headset and pantyhose? Sounds awesome." I called before I could lose my nerve and set up an interview, having no idea the utter humiliation I was in for.

As I pulled up to the strip mall which held the small office, the fluttering in my stomach was starting to feel less like the wings of benign butterflies and more like the sharp stingers of angry hornets, an anxious foreshadowing of the upcoming events. Undeterred, I walked into the tiny room and introduced myself. The look of amusement on the face of the receptionist should have been my cue to turn around and walk out, but I come from a stubborn lot and so I stayed. Less than five minutes later I was in my car holding back tears after having been informed that I was too short, too pale, too redheaded, and too small-breasted. It was back to the cubicle with me.

A few months later, having repaired most of the damage to my ego, and once again thinking of ways I could avoid going to my job, I gathered up the courage to respond to another ad. This one was for a waitress at a nude strip club. I was hired on the spot, with one little catch. It was a topless position. I would serve drinks, and also be on the stage list, but only to go topless and not fully nude. I never personally had any issue with nudity, so the topless part was easy; the dancing, not so much. Although I was technically hired, I would have to meet the owner and submit to a viewing.

His office was located in the back of the club between two large stages. As I walked through the door, I was faced with a multi-faceted odor which contained hints of whiskey and old farts. The owner himself proudly displayed the symbols of a motorcycle club, although his appearance alone would have been enough to guess that he had long ago given up his aspirations of climbing the corporate ladder. An older waitress who would later serve as my mentor, had come into the room with me. She introduced me and then told me to take off my clothes. I did as I was asked and was rewarded with this statement, "Boobs are kinda small, but you're pretty hot" from the grizzled old biker. My new mentor told me later that this was quite a compliment. At eighteen, I had not yet realized that an off-handed compliment from an aging biker would be the foundation for a sense of confidence that would serve me quite well over the next twenty years. I would also learn later that this experience had also taught me the value of taking a risk.

Another risk strippers face is being criticized for being in the profession itself. Being judged or rejected based on physical appearance is one thing, sitting at the Thanksgiving dinner table across from your dad is a whole other deal. Strippers have to decide whether to keep their jobs secret, or to be open and accept the backlash from family, friends, and anyone else who may disapprove. I pretended to be a waitress for about a month after making the transition from waitress to dancer, before deciding that I didn't like lying about it. I decided that if I was going to be a stripper, hiding it would be hypocritical. If I was going to expose myself literally, I wasn't going to do it half-assed by lying about it. I couldn't truly accept myself if I was going to lie to everyone. Being honest about the choice I made to become a stripper also removed the possibility of the secret being exposed by someone else. Thus, removing the leverage such a person might think they had.

Shortly after I started stripping, the entirety of the football team from the high school I had attended ended up in the very club where I was working. Although I was born in Southern California, I had moved to a tiny town in the middle of the Sierra foothills with my mom when I was 10. Having never completely adjusted to small town life, I was not what you might describe as popular. Because of my smart-ass reputation, I was always at odds with the cool kids, which definitely included the football team and their groupie cheerleader counterparts. That being the case, these guys were delighted to see me. They reveled in the fact that they had caught me doing something dirty and would get to tell the whole town, resulting in my complete and utter embarrassment. But alas, the joke was on them. I had already told my family, thereby removing any and all gossipy ammunition they thought they had. Unfortunately, the English teacher's daughter was also on the dance list that night and having not told anyone about her new career, was not as lucky. Her parents found out the hard way.

Being honest did not eliminate all of the concern from my family. Coming from a Catholic background, my stripping was difficult for them at first. Fortunately for me, both of my parents were self-employed and understood my need for independence from traditional employment. I was also able to point out that with the income I was making, it was highly unlikely that I would be calling to ask for money. Funny how money can override fundamental religious values.

Risks cannot for all intents and purposes be avoided, but the risks we choose to take should be considered carefully. Like jumping off a cliff, bridge, or out of a plane, some risks we choose simply to enrich our lives, while other risks we have to take simply to keep living.

Learning to take risks is really about overcoming anxiety. Sometimes that anxiety is warranted, but much of the time it's just an irrational fear. Our brains are expressly wired to keep us alive, and that's why we tend to get anxious about some things that are for the most part safe. I went on a zip line for the first time a few years ago, and although my brain kept telling me that I would die, I knew that in reality it was safe. The trick was convincing my brain that I would be OK. Once I let go and started moving, it was exhilarating, despite the fact that I kept picturing myself plummeting to my death, or the harness rupturing a breast implant at the end of the line. All of those fears were ultimately deemed irrational. If I had given in to them, I would've missed that experience, and my husband would've had fun calling me a pussy for the rest of the trip. If and when I do it again, I will likely experience the same anxiety, but to a lesser degree.

Every time we overcome the anxiety that comes with taking a risk, we make ourselves stronger and more resilient. Most of the time it takes practice, and what is described as exposure therapy, to become immune to the automatic responses from the part of the brain that keeps telling us we are facing certain death. So, the best way to eliminate that response is to keep doing it. If you're afraid of spiders, for instance, get closer and closer to one with a flip flop, until you are brave enough to smack it. After enough time, you should be able to see a spider without the rush of adrenaline that sends you screaming in the other direction.

In my case, being on stage made me want to puke the first few times. After a while, I looked forward to being on stage, and eventually grew to really enjoy it. (In the interest of full disclosure, applause and money helped a lot; admittedly, you may not be showered with money when you smack a spider with a flip flop.) When I think about what my life would've been like had I not overcome that fear of the stage, I am really grateful that I did. Another benefit is that while I didn't meet my husband in the club, being exposed to so many men helped me see a good one when I found him. The risk I took when I decided to start stripping facilitated all the good things in my life I have now.

Writing may have been the most difficult risk I have ever taken. While stripping might seem like a bigger risk, honestly speaking, the thought of people judging what I had to say brought on even more anxiety than the fear of being booed off stage. I know most people think strippers are stupid. And while some of them are quite stupid, likely in direct proportion to the larger population, the stereotype persists. That brought on the thought that my writing would be considered stupid, too. In fact, my early attempts were mostly fiction and terrible. Despite this fear, I kept doing it. I eventually became better at it and have for the most part become comfortable with the constructive criticism I receive. Once again, I am glad I faced that fear and got the fuck over it.

Whether it be confronting a big hairy spider, bungee jumping, or asking your boss for a raise, facing your fears takes practice. Simply doing it once isn't enough. Fear fades gradually, not all at once. If you finally decide to jump out of a plane for the first time, that's great, but you will still be scared the next time, just not as much. Repetition is the only way to conquer fear once and for all. The good news is that it does get easier, a little bit at a time. Almost any fear can be resolved if you keep at it.

Now that you know taking risks is important, how do you decide which risks are worth taking? Well, the first thing is to dig really deep inside and think of the things you really want. In my case, growing up thinking I was ugly, I wanted to feel pretty. Stripping gave that to me. I've always loved to read, although mostly horror, and I secretly always wanted to put my own words on paper. For a time, I didn't feel confident that I could do either one, they both felt incredibly risky. Figuring out what you really want for yourself is the first step. While a terrible cliché, follow your dreams.

If you dream of being an actor or model, maybe check out an autobiography about someone you admire. Maybe you have an idea for an invention – take a look, see what's out there. If you start to explore and begin to flesh out your desires, you may find that they aren't as unattainable as you may think. Could you imagine if Tom Hanks gave in to his own doubts about acting? The world might be just a little darker. We all needed a little Gump in our lives. He took a risk making that happen for us. That first little step could be all you need to realize your dream. But it's a risk. You could fail miserably, like my attempts at fiction. Keep trying. Even failed attempts mean progress. Failure is far better than to have never tried at all. How will you know if you could've been the next Lady Gaga if you don't risk getting up and singing a little karaoke? Not taking those kinds of risks leads to regret, and that, my friends, is the real bummer.

There are some risks that really are dangerous and probably not worth taking. Hitchhiking, two week old potato salad, and creepy Uncle Lester's offer to babysit for free might be a few. If you've always wanted to skydive, instead of just making an appointment with the first company that comes up on Google, maybe take a deeper look into their reputation. If there seems to be a disproportionate amount of deaths, or the owner has a history of DUI's, maybe take a look at the second one on the list. You will feel more comfortable with whatever risk you are deciding to take if you are well informed and prepared. Information won't completely alleviate your anxiety, but it's a good start. You may still shit yourself on the way down, but if you've done your homework, you'll more likely live.

Risks are what make our lives rich and meaningful. Don't take it from me, take it from SpongeBob, who eventually decided that going outside his pineapple was a risk worth taking.

Chapter 3

You Took a Risk - Now What?

How to Handle Risks That Feel Like Failures

It's been a long night and you are starving. As you walk into the dressing room, your coworker sees you glance at the sushi roll sitting on the dressing room counter. She very generously offers it to you. You hesitate. Without going through the trouble of carbon dating, you really don't have any idea just how old this sushi roll may actually be. However, it is still in its plastic clamshell, so how risky could it really be? It is likely to be at least slightly younger than the dusty junk food in the dressing room snack machine. The only place open this time of night is Denny's or fast food, and you've been trying to eat healthier. "Fuck it," you think and accept her offer. As you scarf the tepid raw fish and rice, you remember that last week you got into a little unresolved argument with this girl. The girl who just now seemed to do you a favor. You start to wonder if your hunger blinded you to the fact that eating what could be an elderly sushi roll, given to you by someone who possibly has a grudge against you, might not be the best idea.

Two and a half hours later, that inner voice that told you this may not be a risk worth taking is proved correct. It seems you're going to miss a few hours of work, with most of it spent praying to the club's suspiciously stained porcelain god. You miscalculated, and you are now faced with the consequences. You took a risk, and it failed.

Or did it? Will you ever make that mistake again? Most likely not. You have learned a hard and painful lesson. Therefore you did not fail. You made progress. Lessons learned are progress, and progress is not failure. We've established that risks are an important part of a fulfilling life, but what happens when they don't turn out the way we want? What do you do when you fuck up? There are really two ways to handle them.

In the case of the toxic sushi, you could call out the girl, scream and yell at her, and possibly lose your job in the process. You can then escalate the issue by making a complaint to the manager or owner, demanding that she be fired instead. You could even file a small claims case and wait for a court date where you can pitch your damages to a judge who probably has little to no interest in your plight, vastly prolonging the situation. Or maybe, roll with me here, you pull your head out of the toilet, take some Tums and laugh it off, knowing that you'll never do that again.

The first option will undoubtedly make you even more angry and upset than you were in the first place, leaving you to wallow in the stink of your own failure. A genuine failure. The second option is to acknowledge you fucked up and place it in the "lessons learned" file somewhere in the back of your brain. Progress.

Sometimes even understanding that you made progress or learned a lesson from your mistake isn't enough to stop the negative thoughts your brain may simply insist on pursuing. It can be hard to accept it when it feels like you failed. As a stripper and not a psychologist, I may not be the most qualified person to help with this problem. There have been times when I have done something for which I can't seem to forgive myself. The best advice I can give would be that you're not alone in this kind of thinking. Seeking support from friends or family can help you put things in perspective. After all, the likelihood that everyone you know has never done anything they regret is simply not possible. A little compassion from someone who can relate may help you show a little compassion toward yourself. As difficult as it may seem, the best way I have found to deal with a risk gone bad is to look for the positive that can be derived from it, even if the only positive is that you won't do it again.

Taking risks can enrich our lives whether they work out or not. Sometimes, the risks we take can enrich others' lives as well. I'm pretty sure I've given a lap dance or two that may qualify as an enriching experience, but I digress. Risks that don't turn out the way you hoped can be a lesson leading to better choices in the future if we make the choice to learn from them. Some people believe that failures are some god's way of sending you a message. It seems to me that a god who sends a message through projectile vomiting and diarrhea is kind of a dick, and frankly should find better ways to fill his or her time. Feeding starving children might be a good start.

You made a choice, took a risk, and now that is a piece of your collective information. No supernatural explanations needed. When you decide to take a risk, you acknowledge that choice and that the outcome is almost never guaranteed. If we knew without a doubt that things would work out every time, it, by definition, wouldn't be a risk.

Failing to be Normal

As my dancing career progressed, I was constantly plagued with the idea that I couldn't do it forever. At some point I would need a normal job. As I watched older dancers deteriorate, I thought I needed to have some sort of a backup plan for the day when no one would want to see me naked. I was highly aware from the very beginning that this would not be a long-term gig. Obviously, after twenty years, I was terribly mistaken on this point, as twenty years might be considered long term.

I started taking classes at a community college right after graduating high school but dropped out shortly after I started stripping. I figured I could correct this by going back to school. Once I had thought I wanted to be a lawyer. After a few years of dancing, and meeting hundreds of lawyers, I no longer wanted to be one. I did like to bake though. I enjoyed being in the kitchen, and also have a wicked sweet tooth. A certificate in baking and pastry arts from the top culinary school in the country was the obvious choice.

I secured my funding and spent eight months covered in flour, sugar, and chocolate. I graduated with a 3.5 GPA (sculpting sugar proved to be my Achilles' heel) and set about finding a job. Thanks to my school's placement program, I was offered a job right away, which I promptly turned down. Why? It turned out that pastry chefs don't make nearly as much money as strippers, and I now had a twenty-thousand-dollar school loan. I took a risk and I failed.

Despite the fact that I now possessed the skills to make everything from scratch baked bread to multi-tiered wedding cakes, I felt like a failure. In my excitement to create a contingency plan for the end of my stripping career, I failed to research how much pastry chefs actually make. Still, I made a few attempts at working as a pastry chef, all ending with the same result. I didn't make enough money, worked too many hours, and grew to dislike working with co-workers, although that probably says more about me than them. The first thing I learned from this whole experience was that I make a miserable and shitty employee. I was far happier as an independent contractor, despite the persistent fear that one day they just wouldn't let me back in the strip club, at least not as a performer.

As my certificate collected dust, there were times when my education came in handy, like when my husband was diagnosed with thyroid cancer. He had to be on a specific diet. Everything he ate needed to be unprocessed, which I was trained to produce. Or when our son and various friends and family had spectacular birthday cakes and specialty desserts made for them at no cost. In some circles, my Christmas cookies are the stuff of legends. Also, through my formal training as well as the training I received at the handful of restaurants where I briefly worked, I learned to limit waste, budget, organize, and manage a successful kitchen. I also learned a lot about savory cooking, which made my weeknight home cooked meals restaurant quality. Still, every month when I received the school loan statement, I reminded myself that I was a failure who wasted twenty thousand dollars. I could've taken a trip to Europe with that money.

For the last seven years or so, my husband and I have hosted Christmas dinner for our friends who otherwise would be spending it at home. It's an event that takes me around a month to plan and at least three days of prep in the kitchen. I look forward to it every year. It is perhaps my favorite social event. On one of these occasions a few years ago, when we were all seated at the table and toasting our friendship, I had a spectacular epiphany. As I looked around at all the guests, every one of them, including my ornery child, had a smile on their face. As their attention turned to their plates, I waited a minute before I started on my own. I realized that not one of these people, some of my favorite people on the planet, thought I was a failure. Or that my culinary education had been a mistake. What I had thought of as a failure for all these years had brought smiles and happiness to all these people I loved. I enjoyed every part of it as well. The planning, the prep, cooking, baking, and decorating. I loved it all. No way this was a failure.

I took a risk which I thought would lead to a new career in culinary arts, and while that aspect of it didn't pan out, there were plenty of things that did. I learned that I loved to cook and bake, and that those skills can be used to help people. My risk not only enriched my own life through new skills, but also the lives of the people I care about. I did not fail. The money I spent wasn't wasted after all. Not. One. Single. Penny.

Some Risks You Can't Choose

There are some times when we take risks without knowing it. For instance, no matter how much I think I know a guy before I take him into the VIP room for a lap dance, I'm taking a risk. He could be wearing a lacy teddy or have an urge to strangle me. I really don't know. While most of the guys are harmless, even the ones with weird fetishes, there have been a few who have been a genuine risk. A few years ago, when working in Reno, I went into a private VIP room for a prepaid hour with a customer who was pretty hammered. It had been kind of a rough night and an hour in the VIP room paid well, so even though I was a little reluctant, given this guy's level of intoxication, I went in. After about thirty minutes, this guy started to get a little – OK maybe more than a little – frustrated with the fact that I was just a dancer and not a prostitute. Out of the blue, he picked me up, flipped me over, and pinned me on the couch. He was laughing and pretending it was a joke. I'm still not sure whether he meant any real harm. In fact, I tend to think not, but he could've killed me. There was a mantle over a faux fireplace with a sharp corner that I could've easily hit my head on. Although there were cameras in each room, and there was only a curtain and not a solid door, no one was looking at the camera at the time. No security tossed the curtain aside to come in to help me. I was alone with this drunk customer. I could've been strangled or worse.

I knew that dancing came with inherent risks, but those risks are supposed to be mitigated by the security in the clubs. In this instance, I didn't know that I wasn't being watched. I was able to get out of the situation unharmed (and paid), but I never returned to that club. Now that I understood that the risk I was taking included not knowing if I could count on security to help me, I was no longer willing to take the risk of working there. The most disappointing thing about that situation was that the club where it happened was a higher end club. They had a cigar bar and a four-star restaurant, but their security didn't match their amenities. Lesson learned, progress made. I wasn't ever that fond of Reno, anyway.

My husband is a great example of how to use an unanticipated risk for his own benefit. When he started work with a telecommunications company that required him to climb high towers, he knew he was risking a potentially deadly fall. In fact, being a tower hand is considered one of the most dangerous jobs in the world. He did not, however, anticipate the effects of high doses of radio frequencies on his body. He developed thyroid cancer. There have not been extensive studies on telecom tower climbers specifically, but the researcher I spoke with from the World Health Organization, after his diagnosis, said it was highly likely that his RF exposure is what caused his cancer. The high incidence of thyroid cancers in tower hands also suggests this to be the case.

If he had known that this was a risk he was taking when he started in the industry, would he have still taken the job? Probably. It was a great opportunity at the time. After his cancer diagnosis and treatment, he didn't quit. Quite the contrary. Instead of letting this unforeseen risk and potential failure halt the progress in his career, he used it to his advantage. Although he was unable to climb towers, he was able to transfer his skills to the management side of the industry which actually paid much better.

Some of you may already know, but cancer, even a highly treatable one like thyroid, is a huge downer. The physical effects are obviously hard, but the mental, emotional, financial, and general stress on a relationship are probably the worst. If it hadn't been for his capacity to pull his dick out of the dirt and deal with it constructively, both of our lives would've almost certainly taken a turn for the worse. I am happy to note that although he is now missing his thyroid and several lymph nodes, he has been cancer

18

free for five years. Occasionally, he is even able to show off his exceptional climbing skills to a new generation of tower hands. I couldn't be prouder of the badass I married. Some risks we choose, and some come unexpectedly. Either way they can be an opportunity to learn and grow. Not everything can be considered to be strictly a success or failure, it ultimately depends on how you deal with it.

When we take a risk that seems like a mistake or a bad choice, it often can be used for the better. The lessons we learn are the important part. Ultimately, it's our choice to let a perceived failure be a blight on our lives or make our lives better, even if the only thing we get out of it is to not make that choice again. By the way, if you happen to run across sushi sitting on a strip club dressing room counter, offered by a girl who probably doesn't like you, you're probably better off grabbing fast food.

Chapter 4

Corrosion of Conformity

The Hidden Danger of Conforming

As little kids, our toys talked to us, at least mine did. Especially my Barbie doll. She told me that I wanted to be just like her. That I wanted to live in a big pink mansion, drive a pink convertible, and that I wanted to be tall, skinny, and blond, just like her. Barbie wanted me to conform because that's what would make me happy and successful in life. For a good portion of my childhood I believed her.

The TV shows, movies, and toys we were exposed to as kids all presented us with an image to aspire to. Growing up in 1980s sunny Southern California, it was a foregone conclusion that I would grow up to be blond, skinny, and married to a successful stockbroker. It didn't take long before I realized that my Barbie doll was portraying an image that I would never live up to. I only had to look in the mirror to understand that she was lying to me.

Cursed with carrot orange hair, freckles, and a nose that appeared alien to the rest of my face, nothing I saw around me told me those things were pretty. My older teenage sister used a pair of pliers to pull up the zipper on her unbelievably tight jeans creating the startling effect of a stuffed sausage. She was attempting to live up to the standards of beauty that she had been taught.

Unless you happen to be born to look naturally like the images we see, you might have been made to feel just a little inadequate, too. Because so many of us don't organically fit the typical standards of beauty, just being yourself can be a risk. By not conforming to what other people think we should look or act like, we are risking judgement and rejection. On the other hand, if we strive to be what we think others want us to be we are denying who we really are. Either way is risky, and either way is ultimately a difficult way to live. One of the reasons I think I chose the path I did was to prove that I could be different and still be considered pretty. I needed to prove to myself that I didn't have to conform. Except I ended up conforming anyway, even though I thought I was rebelling. It took a real-life Barbie to show me how wrong I was.

A Real-Life Barbie

I thought that when I started dancing, I had become comfortable with the fact that I wasn't "Barbie" perfect. A glaring indication that I was not comfortable with my looks was that I was jealous of girls I thought were perfect. As a dancer, it wasn't just the movies and magazines that told me I wasn't quite up to par, it was the girls with whom I was directly competing. My unfortunate initial reaction to this was to make anyone whom I found intimidating as uncomfortable as I possibly could. There was one girl in particular who caused my ego to be threatened quite severely. She had blond hair down to her ankles, a perfect pair of tits, and impeccable makeup, so naturally I wanted to punch her in the face.

I had made it all through school using my mouth as a weapon. I had never been in a physical fight. I didn't even know how to throw a punch. So, when I found myself in the throes of envy, I pulled out my most effective offense, my words. I walked right up to this beauty queen and asked her how in the hell she wiped her ass with all that hair. Luckily for me, she was just as insecure as I was and didn't react violently. In fact, she dropped her gaze and seemed to acknowledge that her hair was ridiculously long and that she had a crooked nose to boot. This unpleasant exchange ended in a friendship or ho-mance that would last a long time, much too long, in fact.

This girl who, as it would happen, went by the stage name Barbie, was very skilled in the art of conforming to what other people thought she should look like. I learned later that she had attended beauty school and had even been in a few pageants. She learned to hide her imperfections with makeup. While I had learned to simply apply a little here and there, she was able to teach me the ins and outs of hiding my freckles, plucking my blond but substantial eyebrows, and even grooming my unruly pubic hair. By the time she was done with me, I looked like a typical stripper.

I not only followed Barbie's advice, but I let her completely control my stripper image. She carried her costumes around in a roll away suitcase and loved to dress me up as her own little doll. Because I was so caught up in my admiration for her looks, I let her make me up as she pleased, even at the expense of my own tastes. Barbie was obsessed with Janis Joplin, so I found myself on stage in aggressively ugly fluorescent bell bottoms dancing to "Piece of My Heart", although my own heart wanted to dance to Metallica. I cowered to her whims despite the fact that I didn't like the way I looked. My lack of self-esteem led me to delude myself that I needed to look the way Barbie wanted me to, not unlike the doll I had as a little girl. The whole time I was telling myself that this was what I wanted, she not only influenced my looks, but my thoughts about myself as well.

Perhaps the best thing that could've happened to my image was Barbie leaving the profession to pursue a job as a restaurant hostess, and eventually a life as an administrative assistant. She tried to convince me to do the same, but because I had started to make money as a dancer and was enjoying the freedom it gave me, I was able to resist her influence. Without my Barbie consistently reminding me of my ugliness I was finally able to indulge my own tastes. I was a metal head at heart, I liked wearing black, I liked spikes and chains. I blossomed as a death metal stripper and although I scared a few people, I was finally free to be the dark and dangerous stripper I always wanted to be.

I was able to break free of Barbie's control in my professional life, but as my "bestie" she still controlled the way I dressed in my real life. I didn't buy one piece of clothing that I thought she might not approve. I was highly aware of and took to heart any minor criticism she may have had toward my looks. Her love of 1980s music and style permeated her life and mine. I lived in fear of her judgement well into my adulthood.

23

Our relationship came to an end after nearly two decades when on a weekend trip to her parents' cabin in the mountains she crossed a line. She criticized my then 5-year-old son's eyebrows. Both my husband and I have very voluminous eyebrows when not managed properly, so our son was doomed to inherit this trait. Grooming his eyebrows at that age was never a consideration for my husband and me. Barbie informed me that it should be considered child abuse to let him go in public with eyebrows like that. While never really willing or able to defend my own looks in her presence, I could not hold back with this kind of insult to my crotch fruit. We got in a huge fight, and after several nasty text exchanges, we haven't spoken since.

Ridding myself of this ball and chain, really the only abusive relationship I have ever been a part of, was one of the best things that could've happened in my life. Despite actually looking a lot like the doll she had named herself after, she never felt like she herself lived up to that image. Her insecurities led her to judge not only herself unfairly, but everyone else who didn't conform to her idea of beauty. She taught me a lot about how to use makeup and clothing to alter my physical appearance, and she also taught me how destructive jealously can be. Until that point, I didn't understand the kind of influence she had on me, all because I thought she was pretty. She was jealous of my other friends to the point that I would sneak around to hang out with other people, just to avoid her scrutiny. When I told her that I thought I might enjoy writing, she told me it was stupid. Sometimes it's not just the outside world that influences the way we see ourselves. Rather, it can be an individual who can project their own insecurities on us, causing us to be untrue to ourselves.

I've seen many women in my profession who take extreme measures to conform to the ideas of beauty they are presented with. The most common way to do this is plastic surgery. I worked with one woman in particular who demonstrated this, unfortunately, very well. She caught my attention when I noticed that she would just pull her boobs out of her bra on stage without actually taking her bra off. This is common when someone has boobs that don't sit up quite high enough unsupported. I could tell that she had breast implants that were likely over the muscle. Most breast implants done today are done under the pectoral muscle, to provide coverage and support to the implant. When they are done over the muscle, the weight of the implant can cause the skin to stretch and the breast to sag. Also, without enough tissue to cover the implant, you can have what is called rippling, where you can see the implant through the skin. In the dressing room, without her bra I could see that she had both of these issues.

That wasn't even the most alarming part of the plastic surgery she had. She also had what appeared to be breast implants in her butt. When she bent over, she had two large mounds that sat high on her buttocks and moved independently of each other, and also independently of her natural tissue. They looked like hamburger buns. I never asked her directly what she had done, but I was in the dressing room when one of the other women had the balls to ask. I heard her say that she had gone to Mexico to have breast and butt augmentation. They had indeed placed her breast implants over the muscle and had also put breast implants in her butt. Breast implants are not designed to be put anywhere except the breast. While there are butt implants, most butt augmentation is done by fat transfer, which is exactly what it sounds like. The doctor will perform liposuction, and then inject that fat into the butt.

Going to Mexico is a common way to lower the cost associated with plastic surgery. It's a terrible idea and a great way to end up with an infection or botched operation. When I heard this lady say that she was also a registered nurse, I had to struggle to control my shock. She definitely knew the risks she was taking, but in her desire to conform to the beauty standards (looking at you JLo), she took the risk anyway.

After I had my son, I struggled with getting breast augmentation myself. After much research I went ahead with it. I am happy with my results, but I do wonder if I myself was pressured to conform to cultural beauty standards. A consequence of my chosen profession is that my idea of beauty is not only influenced by culture but also what I am competing with. My sense of what looks good is a little warped. Some people may look at a porn star's makeup and think, "Wow, she looks like a whore", while my thought is more like, "Wow, how can I look more like a whore?" Obviously, my perspective is skewed. Thankfully, in my life outside of the strip club, I am happy just to look like myself and don't tend to exaggerate my look. Because I felt ugly as a kid, for me the need to conform my looks to the standards I saw in culture and then the strip club was very powerful. I'm not sure most people are compelled to conform in that way as I was. It might be that I'm just a little (or a lot) vain.

Sometimes one of the biggest risks we can take is to not conform to the standards we see, but to just be ourselves. When we deny who or what we are, we are also denying ourselves the chance to be happy and successful. If we constantly feel like we are so different than everybody else and we must put on a façade to find acceptance from others, we aren't living a real life. To speak up or to expose your true feelings to the world can be terrifying. On the other hand, I think that the scariest thing of all is to have lived your life wishing you could've been someone or something else. Not taking that risk is ultimately to risk regret. There are so many places in our lives where we can be pressured to conform. Not just in terms of what we look like, but also in what we are taught to believe.

Sit, Kneel, Stand, Pray

As the last of six kids in my family, by the time I came around my family didn't go to church much anymore. We still went every once in a while, but it seemed to me at the time that it was more to convince themselves that they were still Catholic than because they actually believed in what was taught there. My best friend across the street went with her family every Sunday. Every Sunday. I often found myself annoyed that my Sunday mornings were mostly spent playing by myself, waiting for her to come home. Occasionally, I would go with her, if only to avoid the crushing boredom caused by the lack of cartoons on Sunday morning TV.

I would sit, kneel, and stand, when I was supposed to, and I mouthed the words to the prayers like I was supposed to, but I never really bothered to listen to what was being said. The one thing I knew above all else, was that if I wanted to be able to play with her, I had to conform to the rituals being performed. To give any hint that I really thought this was all crap, at least to a five-year-old, would be to risk a very convenient friendship. She was the only friend I had who lived close enough for me to walk to her house unaccompanied.

26

Even though my family believed in God, they had left most of these rituals behind years before. My parents got divorced right around the time I was born, and although it wasn't her decision, my mother was now unwelcomed in the church she had been raised in. Divorce, whether your decision or not, was not allowed. She still didn't give up her faith. Instead, she sought other denominations that would accept her. I always found this sad. When she needed her faith the most, they had abandoned her, and yet she couldn't let go. Almost like an abusive relationship, she was unable to stop believing. Her need to conform to the beliefs she had grown up with blinded her to the fact that this conformity was in fact harming her.

As a kid I didn't understand a lot of the nuances of religion, I just knew that everybody believed in God, and if I didn't, I risked rejection from my f͏ nd society as a whole. Belief is one of those thing͏ ͏cted to conform to. To reject the idea of ͏ ͏ject what is considered good and ͏ d that certain elements of reason and ͏ ͏ want to fit into the world. Just like ͏ansion, to say, "But I don't want to heresy.

͏nt to be loved and accepted, we ͏re not actually in control of our ͏ controls everything for us and ͏or ourselves. Religion, and ͏ot to believe our own brains ͏ y want us to believe in. We ͏ ͏, but if we use those gifts to ͏ ͏r power, we are evil. What the

͏u need something, pray for it. If it doesn't happen, you ͏ t need it anyway. What if you're starving? God decided you didn't really need food? These are the burning questions we are told not to ask. If you do, you will be punished, but not by a vengeful god, but by the society which wants you to conform to its own ideals.

We conform to avoid ridicule and rejection, but the real risk is in conforming at all. By conforming, we risk losing ourselves. We are essentially lying to ourselves, not only in how we look, but in how we think. How many potentially brilliant scientists were stunted because they conformed to a religious ideology? How much progress have we given up to conformity? What if we simply trusted our own capacity to follow our own ideas instead of conforming to what others tell us to? What have you been missing out on in your life because it doesn't conform to what you were taught?

When we refuse to conform, we threaten those who do conform, and that can leave us feeling alone and isolated. People who feel threatened by someone's refusal to conform the way they have, fear it could expose their own uncomfortable feelings that they may be hiding. If they see you take a stand, their reaction is to reject your assertions. When I decided to stand up to Barbie, it was very difficult for me. In fact, writing about it was difficult for me. I loved her, and I always will, but I came to understand just how toxic our relationship had become. It wasn't until she focused her criticism on my son that I saw I was constantly trying to conform to her ideas of who I should be. I lost a friend, but I found myself. It turned out that the friends I had been neglecting were far more supportive than Barbie had ever been.

When I gave up trying to believe in something that I saw no evidence of, I felt like I was exposed. I felt exposed not only to the reality that I didn't believe as others did, but that I would be found out. Like I had been caught doing something worse than just asking questions. I thought that if it was known that I didn't really believe I would also lose people I cared about. Because the fear of being exposed as a skeptic, agnostic, or atheist to my family and friends was so strong, I kept it hidden for a long time.

What I found when I finally came out was that the people who couldn't handle my curiosity about a world without a god are people who seem to be likely not convinced themselves. Whenever I was presented an argument for the existence of a higher power, it sounded more like they were trying to convince themselves as much as me. Those kinds of conversations usually ended with the assertion that they just had faith or that they just felt it inside. You could almost see the little glimmer of doubt in their eyes. After all, how many times have our feelings been an inaccurate depiction of reality? For example, my mother once took me to emergency because I felt I was dying. The severe stomach pains I was having turned out to be gas, but in the moment, I thought I would die. My feeling of impending death was so strong, I was able to convince my mother I was dying. My feelings were evidence of something, but not death. Our brains are so suggestible, that when we have strong feelings, it can be easy to convince ourselves of things that aren't true.

I think some believers may be clinging to the need to conform out of fear of being rejected, but also just plain fear. Asking uncomfortable questions is made all the more difficult when you are brought up with the threat of eternal torture. The thought of someone watching and judging not only your actions but your inner thoughts is scary. If God hears your prayers, then he also hears your doubts. If someone starts to doubt what they are taught, the fear kicks in and the believer tamps down those thoughts. But the doubt is still there. Penn Jillette describes these doubts as a pebble in your shoe. When you have a pebble in your shoe, there may be times when it rolls into a recess in your shoe and you can't feel it. Inevitably it will roll back under your foot and remind you it's still there. Doubt is like that, too. It may hide for a while, but unless it is addressed head on, it will always remain.

Asking questions can be scary for believers because it might expose the doubts they have been suppressing. Asking yourself challenging questions is the first step in discovering who you really are and what you want to get out of this life. I hope I can show even one of those people I mentioned (maybe you), that it is OK to ask questions, that sometimes those questions might lead you not to a god, but to yourself.

Chapter 5

You're Smarter Than You Think

Critical Thinking Can Be Uncomfortable, But Worth It

Surrounded by identical doors, I padded as quickly and as quietly as I could down an endless hallway. The drab industrial carpet stretched out for miles. I was lost and looking for my niece who was lost, too. That was the whole point. To get lost, and then race each other to get back to the door belonging to my sister. A door which looked exactly like all the rest of the doors. We had to be exceptionally quiet when we played this game. To disturb any of the other occupants of the condominium complex would mean the end.

My oldest sister, who is fourteen years older than I am, had a child in her late teens, which resulted in my becoming an aunt at the ripe old age of 4. My niece and I would for the most part play well together when I would visit her. The hallway game was by far our favorite, as playing with toys would usually end in an argument. The game started at a random place deep in the recesses of the huge multistoried complex. We would then each go a different way then try to beat each other back home. It was fun because all the hallways looked the same. Getting mixed up and turned around was remarkably easy. The elevators weren't much help, either, because they, too, looked the same and would simply dump you off in a hallway that was just like the one you left. This game filled hours of time that would have otherwise been spent yelling about who had the best My Little Ponies. (Spoiler alert: It was me.) I loved this game.

Until my stupid brain ruined it all. On what would turn out to be the last time we played this game, I found myself standing in yet another generic hallway. I could feel time slipping by and was agitated by the thought of losing the round. No matter how many turns I took I kept ending up at the same spot. I could tell by the lonely piece of gum squished into the corner where two beige walls met. In my frustration, my mind started to ponder the grotesque amount of light brown that covered every surface when I noticed something that stuck out. The numbers that marked each door were several shades darker than the rest of the décor. For some reason, the numbers on the doors had never caught my attention before. Now I took a second to consider them. Like all good numbers they were in order, ascending as they went toward the elevator, and descending as they went toward the laundry room. As I began to walk down the hall, I stopped at the elevator and saw that the first number on each door corresponded to the floor I was on. That was when I understood that I could never get lost again. All I had to do was follow the numbers and they would lead me back home. Always. Dejected, I made my way back home. The game was over. I ruined it.

I stood at the door for a full five minutes before my niece showed up, sweating and flustered. She had made too much noise and had gotten yelled at. So naturally, I told her we couldn't play the game anymore because she had been too loud. I know, I'm kind of an asshole. Up until then, simply guessing at random which way to go was the fun part. The knowledge I had gained by applying just a tiny bit of logic ruined it forever. We would have to find something else to do, practically guaranteeing a fight.

I didn't know it at the time, but critical thinking is what ruined my game. Critical thinking, by definition, is the ability to objectively evaluate information generated by observation, experience, and reasoning as a guide to belief or action. Simply applying logic and reason to an obvious, but overlooked, little piece of information spoiled all the fun. When we watch movies, magic tricks, or play games we have to suspend our tendency to use logic and reason or the magic is gone. How entertaining would a zombie movie be if you can't put aside the fact that once a body starts to rot, walking would eventually be impossible? In that case, while gross, zombies aren't much of a threat and there goes all the fun of being scared. The entire plot disintegrates along with the walking dead. That said, learning to think critically is the most important part of dealing with the risks we take in life.

Critically Thinking Stripper

The words above are not usually thought of as going together particularly well. We'll get to stereotypes later. The truth is, I would not have made it out of the sex industry relatively well adjusted without my ability to think critically. In my previous books on stripping, I try to impart to future dancers the importance of staying sober while working. While this is a hugely unpopular opinion, I repeat it because alcohol or other substances severely impair your ability to think critically. Not that I'm against getting hammered occasionally, just not when working in what could be a dangerous environment.

As a dancer, there have been many times when the ability to assess a situation quickly and accurately has come in handy in the strip club, although I practically count on my customers to suspend their own abilities to think critically. Once customers figure out that it's all a charade designed for entertainment purposes only, the jig is usually up. Just like a magician or illusionist, I'm like a slutty version of David Blaine unless they are aware upfront that my act is just that, an act. When and if they figure it out, they are disappointed. Sometimes dangerously so, and that is when I need to be able to evaluate the situation and act accordingly.

On one such occasion, I was in the VIP room with a gentleman who was intent on whispering sweet nothings in my ear. Unfortunately, what he was whispering was neither sweet nor nothing. Whenever I would get my head close to his, he would say in a breathy voice, "I want to suck on your toes." Now, I'm not in my real life into foot stuff. In fact, it really grosses me out. At the time this dance was happening, it was very close to the end of the night, and I was absolutely exhausted. I had up until a certain point not let him know that I was utterly repulsed by his fetish. Whenever he wasn't looking at my face, I couldn't help but crinkle it in disgust, until finally I inadvertently whispered, "eeew." He heard me, and said, "Did you just say eeew?" Fuck. Time to implement a little critical thinking, not wanting to lose any money or really piss off this guy, I said, "No. I said aww, I want to feel your tongue in between my toes." I'm still waiting on my Oscar nomination.

If he had figured out my true feelings, he not only would've been disappointed, but probably embarrassed as well. Not knowing much about this person except his foot fetish, I couldn't really predict the way he might act when his illusion was shattered. I was already really tired, had I been intoxicated on top of that, I might not have been able to defuse the situation. People who feel they have been fooled may not take into consideration at the moment that there are cameras and bouncers watching them. For all the information I had about this person, I had no way of knowing if he might have acted violently, and that is why thinking critically and acting upon the information I did have is so important.

You might be relieved to know that you don't have to be a stripper to think critically. Critical thinking is helpful to everyone in just about any situation. You probably do it most of the time already. Like when that person you vaguely remember from high school messages you on Facebook about an amazing business opportunity. All you have to do after a small initial investment, is get your friends and family to sign up, and then they do the same with their friends, until boom! We're all rich. Chances are, you took a very short amount of time to evaluate the information about this business opportunity and recognized it as a pyramid scheme. Congratulations, you're smarter than you think.

When we willingly suspend our critical thinking skills for the sake of entertainment, it is purely for our enjoyment. Books, movies, and sometimes strippers, present us with fantastic ideas, but if we consider the actual facts and circumstances, we would not be entertained. We would be annoyed. The vast majority of the time, the plots are simply not plausible. I seek out horror books and movies that are mostly impossible in real life, because if I do get really scared, I can logic my way out of my own panic. In the moment, however, considering the character's scary circumstances and how I may react to them are fun to be immersed in.

I don't walk up to random men on the street and pretend to be romantically interested in order to get money out of them. I expect them to understand that they are in the strip club for entertainment only. It even says that on the door to the main entrance of the club. That's the difference between entertainment and outright lying. When someone asks you to suspend your reasoning skills in a situation that could have real life consequences, that's where things get a little tricky.

When your Facebook friend asks you to join a Multi-Level Marketing scheme, and then gets upset when you take the time to investigate the company before getting involved, that person was hoping you would suspend your logic in an effort to make money. They may or may not have convinced themselves that it is a legitimate investment. If they really believe that the opportunity is a valid one, then your asking questions could seem offensive. If they know it's bullshit, then they could get upset at your skepticism because they have been called out on said bullshit. Either way, for your friend your questions are a problem.

That is when the value of critical thinking becomes most apparent. In previous chapters, I talked about the value of taking risks. Applying critical thinking is how you decide which risks you are willing to take. If someone tells you to just have faith or to trust them yet discourages you from asking questions, that's when you need to be on your guard. Asking difficult and sometimes inconvenient questions is the best way to gather data to evaluate the situation before you act.

While a valuable skill, critical thinking will inevitably lead to new knowledge and sometimes that knowledge can have unforeseen consequences. If you decide not to invest in your friend's MLM scheme, they may decide that you don't trust them and maybe commit the ultimate insult of unfriending you. If you find out how the magic trick works, your favorite illusionist may not be nearly as entertaining. But is all that really so bad? The point is to figure out what to question and what to leave as mystery. When strictly for fun, mystery is great. When making a serious life decision, mystery is dangerous.

It is also important to apply critical thinking to our own thoughts. When we start to question certain things about ourselves, it can get a little uncomfortable. OK, a lot uncomfortable. Like why we react or act the way we do sometimes. Asking questions about ourselves gives us that little tingly feeling down below, like why you keep sabotaging otherwise positive relationships, for example. Questioning ourselves might lead to things we are trying to cover up. The things you are afraid to question about yourself are very likely the things that lead to frustration and unhappiness in your life. They are probably what are holding you back from really living your life. Asking questions about yourself sucks but is the only way to get down to what is really making you miserable or holding you back.

When I first started dating, I had a habit of testing my boyfriends to see if they would leave me. I would hint about taking a break, or breaking up, to test if they really wanted to be with me. Finally, my eventual husband told me if I kept doing that, he really would leave me. That led me to question why I felt like I had to constantly seek reassurance that he wouldn't abandon me. When I thought about it, I realized that I was harboring a fear of abandonment because I had felt that my dad left me. I know you're shocked, a stripper with daddy issues. But that was the truth, when I finally confronted that fear I was able to let it go. Twenty years later, my husband is still sticking around. I'm not sure he would have if I had not stopped the behavior that came from an unresolved issue. The questions we are most afraid of knowing the answers to are usually the most important. Although it's hard, when they are finally dealt with, the relief you get is worth it. By finding your own truth through asking hard questions about yourself, you find freedom.

There are some times when we are simply unable to ask ourselves difficult questions. You may need someone's help. Someone who is objective, educated, and experienced in uncovering unresolved issues. Someone who will listen attentively and even take notes. Someone who will help you get to the bottom of self-destructive behavior and confront the things you really might not want to confront. If you haven't figured it out yet, I'm describing a psychologist. If that's a step that freaks you out, that could be your first clue that you need one. There is no shame in getting help - and it's not like you have to tell everyone what you're doing. Keep it to yourself if you have to, but if you think you need it, do it.

If you do decide that you need professional help, I would advise that you keep an open mind, and look for someone you feel works for you. Not every doctor is the right one for you. Getting help from someone you don't like, or you feel doesn't understand you can be worse than no help at all. When I was sent to my first psychologist at age 14, it was the wrong one. She kept talking about herself and her first sexual experiences. She was weird and didn't listen to me at all. When I told her that I was planning to run away, she did nothing. I ran away with a couple of tweakers, who thankfully weren't nearly as bad as they could've been, but the fact that I lived to tell about it (and, *shameless plug alert*, write about it in my first book) is beside the point. She was not a good doctor for me, and probably shouldn't be a doctor at all. If the first doctor you go to isn't doing it for you, try another. There will be one that works for you.

Not only do we need to question ourselves about things that make us uncomfortable or behave in a certain way, we also need to question ourselves about the things that make us feel good. I know that sucks, but, for example, let's say you feel really good seeing something bad happen to someone you're not particularly fond of. That's one time you need to ask yourself why. Sometimes the things that make us feel good in the moment are not really good for us long term, so you need to question them. What is making you want to keep doing those things? Chances are there is a driving force behind it that you may need to examine and deal with. That applies to our behavior and also the information we seek out. If you are only seeking and believing information that you already like or agree with, you are probably being deceived, either by the source or by yourself. Time to question yourself.

Cognitive Dissonance

With the invention of the internet and social media, we are constantly confronted with all sorts of information. Algorithms that try to anticipate what we will want to buy, click on, or like are the driving force behind the information we are exposed to. It seems that the days of casually reading the newspaper and digesting the information objectively are gone. What we see now on our various online platforms is tailored to the history of where we've clicked before. Data gathering and distribution analyze not just what we click on individual sites, but every time we click or scroll anywhere on the internet. That information is used not just for marketing, but sometimes to influence our opinions. Instead of just getting impartial information, we are shown things that are designed to obtain a certain response from us. Sometimes the people or organizations behind this misleading or biased information have nefarious intentions. This means we must not only think critically and question things that seem to be sketchy, but even more important, question those things that seem to confirm the way we already think.

For example, even if I read a headline that closely aligns with opinions I already hold, my first reaction could be, "Wow, I knew it!" but my second reaction should be to consider the source and the information against other sources. Is this from an organization that has an agenda? Is this same information being spun from a different angle elsewhere? Are they trying to sell me something? As tedious as it sounds, it is now very necessary to question information that you really want to believe. If it sounds too good to be true, or if it aggressively reaffirms your beliefs or opinions, you need to question it. The information presented to us online is largely unregulated. It can't always be trusted. You need to use your critical thinking skills to get to the truth, even if it makes you uncomfortable.

The tendency to discount information and activities that uncomfortably challenge our opinions and beliefs is a result of cognitive dissonance, which leads to confirmation bias. If you like to drink to excess, you may seek out information that tells you that alcohol is good for you, but deliberately ignore the part where it says, "in moderation". You are biased toward looking for and only ingesting information that tells you what you want to hear or confirms what you already believe. That will ultimately lead to you creating your own information bubble, which stunts your learning and personal growth. Kind of like believing that the stripper in your lap really likes you, when she could be thinking you're kind of gross.

When we walk into church, we are told to leave our critical thinking skills at the door. Do not dare to question the existence of an omniscient being who stubbornly refuses to show himself. Do not question that you're born a sinner because a woman created out of a man's rib ate an apple she wasn't supposed to. Thinking critically here would be unacceptable and will ultimately lead to a life of sin and eternal damnation. Use your critical thinking anywhere but in church, or you will be sorry, forever. Unfortunately, we are told to have faith when it is not actually warranted or good for us. In the case of religion or belief in a deity, we are told that to be faithless is to insult the very deity we are supposed to believe in. Cognitive dissonance plays a huge role in religious and other supernatural beliefs. They tell us what we want to hear and threaten us if we dare to question. So, how does church differ from your sketchy friend's fantastic skin care line? I don't think it does, except maybe that your friend only unfriends you on social media and doesn't promise to punish you after you're dead.

Seeking the truth about yourself and reality can seem to be a bit of a bummer. However, that is very much not the case, my friend. Opening yourself up to exploring yourself and the world can be one of the most rewarding things you can do in this life. Don't take anyone's word for it, not even mine. Find out on your own how awesome this life can be when you choose to take control of it and learn. It can take some effort, but when you open your eyes to how not only you function but how the world works as well, the results are no less than life changing. Taking the ultimate risk to discover what may be some uncomfortable truths leads us to learning how to live a more fulfilling life. Letting go of the fantasies that kept us from learning is the most liberating thing you can do. Like skinny dipping in the middle of the night, the naked plunge into knowledge is exhilarating.

Chapter 6

God Told Me to Touch Your Pussy

Take Responsibility

It was a dark and stormy night. OK, I don't really remember what the weather was like that night. I do remember it was a Tuesday, and I was sitting across the tiny table from a middle-aged white guy with poorly fitting glasses. He was droning on about his job as a social worker. The only thing that kept me even slightly interested was the fact that he seemed to have an extremely poor opinion of those he was in charge of helping. And the fact that he was talking about being a devout Protestant. I made a casual joke about us not being able to be friends because I had been raised Catholic. Although my joke fell flat, I hung in there. Tuesdays tend to be slow most of the time, so you need to have a little conversation before you can lure someone into the VIP room. Since there aren't usually that many customers on weeknights, you look like kind of an ass if you just ask for a lap dance and then walk away to sit by yourself in the corner. So, I endured this irritatingly bland excuse for a conversation.

This guy carried on about how he went to church and how he did his best to help people in his job, oblivious to the fact that the way he spoke about them was anything but kind. He really felt the need to let me know that he was a good person, and that he let his god show him the way. Nevermind the fact that maybe his church friends might not approve of his spending his Tuesday nights talking with a half-naked red-headed harlot, silly details. After listening to this guy talk about what a great guy he was because of his faith for what seemed like hours, but was really only about ten minutes, I finally got him to go in the back room.

41

The dance started pretty normal, and then got a little weird. While I had been discounting in my head what he had been saying when we were talking, there must have been a part of me that bought his shtick about his faith making him a good guy. I found myself surprised when I felt his hand creeping toward my southern region. I put my hand over his and guided him away from my lady bits, and yet he persisted. Maybe the Protestant god was more lenient than the Catholic one, but this didn't seem consistent with his assertion of being a virtuous fellow. In fact, he became so aggressive in his quest to touch my nether regions, that I ended the dance. Although touching is allowed in some markets, pussy touching is generally frowned upon. For me, it's a boundary I won't cross. If I let every guy who wanted to touch my pussy do so, I would need to have my gynecologist on retainer. He was annoyed but paid me anyway, and I tried to memorize his ultra-generic face so that I wouldn't waste my time with him again.

A little while later I saw a friend of mine, a cute little Latina, come out of the VIP room with the same guy. She had an irritated look on her face. I asked her, "Did you just dance for that dude with the glasses?" She replied, "Yeah, and he kept telling me that God told him to touch my pussy." I put on my best not shocked face.

What God Wants Us to Do

Well, if God says so, it must be the right thing to do. Funny how God seems to know exactly what we want to do and tells us to do so. It's almost like it's what you really want to do, and God just conveniently gives you a reason to do it. Like touching a stripper's pussy. Did God really want him to grope me? What better excuse than an all-good, all-knowing supernatural being who speaks to you through your own thoughts telling you to do something that some people may find offensive or wrong? It's not like anyone can prove that God didn't tell you that. Seems reasonable. Or not.

Unfortunately, God seems to be used as a convenient excuse for all sorts of abhorrent behavior. Either because he explicitly tells you so through a religious text, or because it's what he told you through your prayers. The Protestant god apparently told this guy that touching a stripper's pussy is what he wanted him to do. Yeah, right.

When we want to do something that we know is not right, gods can come in handy. It can be easy to deceive ourselves into believing that our urges or compulsions come not from ourselves but from some outside influence. It doesn't even have to be a supernatural entity. If we doubt our own intentions, we can look to put the responsibility anywhere but ourselves. Your hormones are going crazy, so you ate a dozen donuts at once. Maybe you were influenced by your hormones, but it doesn't negate the fact that you chose to eat a dozen donuts at once. I have done this by the way, and I wouldn't recommend it. I understood, however, that I made that choice, and the fact that I felt like death afterward was my own doing. There may have been physiological or emotional factors that led to it, but I knew that it was my choice. Understanding that I had the power to give in or not to those cravings is what stopped me from doing it again. If I crave donuts now, I don't tell myself that since my period is around the corner, I am helpless from eating a whole box. I understand that while my urge is strong, the choice is still mine. If I don't want to feel like I'm going to die I eat only one donut, maybe two.

Hormones, while compelling, don't leave you choiceless, but maybe God does. If you're taught to believe that there is a higher power that knows better than you, do you really have a choice to ignore his calling? Whatever the feeling you get when you think that God is speaking to you, are you really free to ignore it? How can your earthly sense of right and wrong possibly trump God's? If you're a true believer, it can't. How does one exactly identify whether a god is speaking or compelling you to do something? In a dream? Through your thoughts? How are you supposed to tell the difference between your own thoughts and a god speaking to you? I imagine this gets especially confusing if God is telling you to do something that you know isn't right, but you want to do anyway. It could be, just maybe, that the only one speaking to you is you.

In the case of the would-be pussy toucher, he made himself believe that there was a deity that put this desire in his head, and he must comply. If he is a true believer, then to question his god's motives would be sinful. He may have convinced himself that an all-powerful god was compelling him, and that conveniently made the choice to try to touch pussy not his. He was just following orders. I wish I could say that this is the worst example of people doing awful and inappropriate things in the name of God. It's not. There are countless examples throughout history that prove my point. Murder, rape, slavery, and a multitude of other rotten acts can be traced back to gods telling someone to commit a crime. If some of those people had to admit that their desires originated from their own brains, maybe they wouldn't have done it. If you remove the scapegoat and have to face the fact that you alone are responsible for your own choices, you might think twice about whether to commit those acts. Better to listen to God, and touch the pussy, than to think too hard about it. Although, I will concede, that this guy may not have actually believed that God wanted him to touch pussy. It could very well be that he was counting on the stripper's belief in God to not question his reasoning and allow the violation. You don't necessarily have to believe in the god yourself, if the person you're trying to violate does.

If you are a believer, you may be more willing to accept that someone who tells you they are also of the same faith is honest. If they are a good Christian, you should be able to take them at their word. After my husband and I bought our house, and we were preparing to leave our rental, I had a brief discussion with our landlord about our security deposit. In the past, my experience has been that landlords tend to exaggerate costs and damages in order to keep a larger portion of the deposit. We had a great relationship with this landlord. He told us on more than one occasion that he was glad we took such great care of his property. Although the subject of our faith or religion had never come up, he informed me that he was a good Christian and would treat us fairly. He seemed to assume that we were Christian like he was. I saw no reason to tell him otherwise. He then kept all of our deposit, despite only being entitled to about half of it. I had proof that he was in violation of the law, but because it was not a whole lot of money, and I didn't want the hassle of taking him to court, I didn't formally dispute it. I did send him a lengthy letter in which I provided proof of his violation of the laws of our state, and also questioned the reason he felt like telling me he was a good Christian. Why did he feel the need to tell me that? Was it to convince me that he wasn't going to screw me, or was it to convince himself that he wasn't an asshole? He didn't respond to my inquest.

It's All Part of God's Plan

There is a Christian outreach group that goes to all the clubs in town and tells girls they can be loved and respected. As if you're stripping because nobody loves or respects you. Frankly, I think it is disrespectful to tell people how they feel based on their occupation. Maybe the workers at Wal-Mart feel unloved and that they aren't respected? This local outreach branch is run by a former stripper I worked with when I first started dancing. She talks about God's plan for her. Apparently that plan included her giving blow jobs to strangers and doing copious amounts of hard drugs. When she was dancing, she didn't feel loved and respected I suppose. I think her feelings had more to do with herself than the industry which she blames for those feelings. It couldn't possibly be that she made some bad choices and now is looking for a way to justify those choices, that would be ridiculous. Her attempts to make excuses for her behavior were a large part of my decision to write about the industry in the first place.

Would that mean her promiscuity and drug use are part of her god's plan for me, too? How very considerate of her. I really don't think I would've been as motivated to write my story if I didn't think she was using the industry and God as an excuse for her own behavior. In my time as a stripper, I certainly had the choice to give blow jobs and do drugs, and yet I chose not to. She blames the industry, Satan, and other people influencing her, but never acknowledges the fact that it was all her choice to do those things that made her feel bad. That's it – Satan made me do it so that God could later show me the way.

One of the hardest things to do is to take a long look at ourselves and see that sometimes we make some stupid choices. Choices that can hurt ourselves and others. One way to make you feel better about acting like an asshole is to find a reason for your behavior. God and Satan make perfect scapegoats. If you need permission to do something shitty, Satan made you do it. If you want an excuse for fucking something up, it was God's plan. All your bases are covered; past, present, and future.

In reality, God, Satan, the universe, your zodiac sign, are all just ways of not taking responsibility for your own choices. If you're

Catholic and you screw up or behave like a jerk, all you have to do is ask God for forgiveness. The person or people you may have hurt really don't figure into the equation at all, only God and your eternal soul matter. As long as your chosen deity or higher power forgives you, everyone else's pain was just part of his plan for them. After all, he knows all, created all, and made you the way you are and presumably knew you were going to be a dick in the first place. By removing consideration for the humans who may have been affected by your bad deeds, all you really have to do to achieve absolution is to tell the guy listening to your every thought that you are sorry. Could this be how priests and other religious authority figures justify their sex crimes? Well, God forgave me, and the abuse was just part of his plan for the victim. Maybe that's why problem priests just get relocated and not arrested. God forgave them already, who are you to judge?

In fact, maybe after you did the bad thing to someone, maybe that led your victim to seek God. Now you might be able to justify that the bad thing you did was actually good. If it led your victim to God and ultimately saved their soul from hell, then God's plan makes sense. He simply used you as a way to help that person find salvation. What a great way to justify some pretty fucked up behavior. I hurt you for your own good. They needed to be hurt to find their own path to God. I'm sorry, but I will have to call bullshit on that one.

So, what about when shitty things happen that we really had no control over? Amazingly, that is also part of God's plan for you. What if you're a victim of something that God told someone to do? One way to get over it is to likewise justify the action as just more of God's plan. You got hit by a car, got cancer, or didn't get the job you wanted. That must be part of God's plan, too. It simply was meant to be. It's God's way of teaching me something. It could be, though, that sometimes shitty things just happen, and we have to deal with it. If you didn't get the job, it is probably not because you were meant to do something else. It could be that there was a more qualified candidate, or that you don't interview well. It sure feels better to put the blame on a bigger plan for you than to simply be better prepared for the job you want. God really comes in handy here, too. He lets you off the hook from your own responsibility. Instead of just saying wow, that sucked, you get to say, well, it just wasn't meant to be.

My husband has very nearly died at least seven times since I met him. He's been electrocuted, fallen 30 feet, been stabbed, had a gun pulled on him, was hit in the face with a large tow hook, had cancer, and has been in several serious car accidents. He's still kicking. Maybe God was trying to tell him something? Like, look what I've done for you in saving your life. Or, believe in me, or next time you'll really die. Stubbornly, he remains an agnostic atheist. Not once in all those times, did he think there was divine intervention. Each mishap can be logically explained using earthly information.

He could have used any one of those near-death experiences as a reason to say there was some divine plan for him. He has simply been in dangerous situations in his quest to support our son and me, and he understands that those were his choices. Some of the situations he knew ahead of time were dangerous. Sometimes he found out the hard way. When he worked as a repossession agent, he was highly aware that he would be upsetting people. In one case, a person decided to stab him. I could take credit for saving his life that time – as a pastry chef, I helped provide some of that tummy cushion that stopped the blade from penetrating too deeply. After a few scary incidences, he changed professions. Albeit, to one that was just as dangerous, but no one in telecommunications has tried to stab him just yet. Sometimes the choices we make put us in situations that can be hazardous. Whether or not we survive them depends on many factors, but a god's plan is not one of them.

Looking to supernatural sources to explain the things that happen in life is in reality just a cop out. In using an excuse that can't be proven one way or another, you are able to do whatever you want and put the blame elsewhere. You and only you are responsible for your choices. It is up to you to make a plan for your life and to find meaning in it. This can be difficult to accept if you have been using God as an excuse for your whole life. You have the power of choice. You choose the things that you can control in life, and you also choose how you react to the things you can't control. Once you understand that the active agent is you, and you alone, who is in control of the choices you make, the world looks a little different.

Instead of thinking, "Well, that job I wanted wasn't meant to be" and give up, now you are free to understand that you can get that job. You are now free to investigate the reasons you didn't get it, and work on those things. Do you lack experience, or maybe your resume needed a little more polishing? You don't have to accept that it wasn't meant to be. You have the power to make it meant to be. It just takes some more work. Anything you want to do, you are meant to do, if you want to put in the effort.

Once you see that you are in control of your life, you are able to overcome your setbacks and do the things that will get you where you want. You are no longer at the mercy of someone else's secret plan. Now the plan for your life is yours. Since it appears that God's plan for so many people includes all sorts of fucked up things, the plan you decide for yourself is bound to be far better. If God's plan for a kid is to be molested by a priest, then fuck that plan, and fuck that priest.

And just in case I haven't been clear, it is never OK to touch another person's genitals without express permission. No matter who or what tells you to.

Chapter 7

Eat the Apple, I Dare You

Seek Knowledge

Once upon a time, actually the first time ever, there was a lush and beautiful garden. This garden and the entire world were created by a powerful being. This being, having created and designed everything in the world and the universe beyond, knows everything, past, present, and future. The only being in existence, we'll call him Jim, was lonely. Jim decided he would make another being just like him to keep him company and to care for this paradise he had made. He gathered up a handful of dirt and made a man we'll call Brad.

Brad's first task was to name the other life forms, called animals, that Jim had made. He was brought each one and gave it a name. And although he had been made to keep his creator company, Brad was lonely, too. So, after he fell asleep, Jim took a rib from him and made a companion, a woman. Brad named her Angelina. Now we have two people made in our all-knowing, all-powerful being's image. Except for one little detail: They were not all-knowing as their creator was.

Jim had created many trees with fruits for Brad and Angelina to eat (diarrhea didn't exist yet), but also put a tree right in the middle of the garden from which Brad and Angelina were forbidden to eat. Jim told them that if they were to eat the fruit, some say it was an apple, from this tree, they would have knowledge of good and evil and would die. Now, as the first people ever, Brad and Angelina were a little naïve, which was exactly the way that Jim wanted them to be.

One day, while Angelina was collecting fruit, she heard a voice behind her that was neither Jim's nor Brad's. She turned and saw that it was a snake. This snake was telling her that she should eat from the forbidden tree, and then she would have the same knowledge as Jim. Being the ignorant person she was made to be, she plucked the apple off the tree and brought it back to Brad. They both took a bite, and the shit hit the fan that had yet to be invented.

Instantly they both understood that they had royally fucked up. They took the word of the talking snake that Jim had created. They ate the fruit that Jim had put in the garden specifically so that he could tell them not to eat it. Brad and Angelina saw that they were naked, and that was wrong for some reason not clearly defined. Jim was pissed. He told Brad that his days of freeloading were effectively over and that he would have to work for the rest of his life, which now had a time limit placed on it. As for Angelina, well, she would be doomed to a life of subservience to her counterpart with the penis. Angelina and all the women after her would be cursed to bleed once a month, with the bleeding to be preceded with irrational cravings for all the foods that would make her fat. She and all the women who came after her would also be cursed to experience excruciating pain during childbirth in addition to unsightly stretch marks. Jim had a knack for creating curses.

The snake, it seemed, was also cursed, despite the fact that he appears to have done exactly what he was made to do; tempting Angelina to eat the fruit of knowledge. Now the snake would become the grossest animal on earth, second only to the overweight man in the middle of a midlife crisis who can't seem to understand that his money doesn't make him any less sexually repulsive. As a person who has an intense dislike for snakes, I can't help but feel that the snake got railroaded in this whole mess.

In addition to creating the universe, earth, and life, Jim also manufactured what we know as original sin. He concocted a plan to make sure that the lives he created would have a reason to fear and obey him. All his creations would now suffer during their earthly lives, but if they choose to love and obey him, he will make sure they get to go to paradise when they die. Jim made it clear that whether or not you choose to love and accept him, in this life you will suffer, regardless. If you choose to ignore him, you will suffer not only on earth but also in a fiery realm of eternal torture in your afterlife. Thanks a lot, Jim.

Malignant narcissism is a psychological syndrome which includes an extreme mix of self-absorption, anti-social behavior, and sadism. Considering the setup perpetrated on poor Brad, Angelina, and the snake, I think it's safe to call Jim a malignant narcissist. In other words, he's kind of a fucking asshole, and all humankind will now pay for it forever.

Out of the three victims in our story, Angelina seems to get it the worst. Sure, Brad has to work and toil for a living, and the snake is, well, gross, but Angelina bears most of the responsibility for the fall of man. I'm not saying that this whole thing didn't make it suck for everyone, but I felt my hips move apart as I was giving birth, and that certainly seemed a little worse than planting tomatoes in the garden. As a cursed woman, I'm not a huge fan of Jim.

Thank Jim for the Strip Club

One of the first things these unfortunate people learned when they ate the forbidden fruit was that they were naked, and that was bad. When I learned this story in Sunday school, I will have to admit I was more focused on the graham crackers and milk that was provided than the actual meaning of the story. In preparation for this chapter, I read the story again. I was unable to understand why they thought it was wrong to be naked. If the first people were made in God's image, then what is wrong with their bodies? Is it wrong for God to be naked, too? What is it about our bodies and genitals that is so wrong in the first place?

This story parallels many other religious texts and myths. The common theme in these stories is that women are temptresses. There is the story of Pandora, who refused the warning not to open the jar of evils, thereby bringing an end to the golden age of man. Sirens luring unwitting sailors to their deaths, and even Helen who is credited with sparking the Trojan War. Women will use their bodies to entice men into doing bad things. The female form itself is apparently so irresistible to men that in some cultures, women must cover up their bodies. The nun's habit and the Muslim hijab are two such examples. Are men so weak that they can't see a woman's hair or ankles without going into an uncontrollable lustful fugue state where they are no longer responsible for their actions? That seems to be the logic at work here, or illogic as the case may be.

For that reason, women must be controlled. "I shall not suffer a woman to teach" is written in the bible. If a woman were to stand up and teach the bible, I suppose men would suffer. I know I suffer when anyone teaches the bible, regardless of which gender they belong to. By putting the responsibility of the fall of man and the original sin on women, some men are willing to use that to their advantage. Since women are lustful creatures who seek to lead men to temptation, it's probably a good idea to not let them have any power. Let's just keep them pregnant and in the kitchen. After all, in the bible, the word rib was loosely translated. Some say it really meant appendage, and what does an appendage do? Well, it's an extension or tool. It's attached to something and is used like a tool. If a woman is made from a man's appendage, then effectively she is his to be used. Not really a separate entity, just an attachment. That makes women more like the pasta attachment that came with my stand mixer, as opposed to the mixer itself. This whole story seems suspiciously like a way to subjugate half the world's population. I wonder what it would've been like if it had been a woman who wrote these stories. Would men then be considered the appendage? I kind of like where that thought is going but let me get back on track.

Religion says sex is shameful. We are supposed to be embarrassed about being naked. Women in particular are supposed to keep their sexuality on the down low. Don't get me wrong, men get their share of guilt and shame, too. But for the most part, women aren't out bragging how much dick they get. You are unlikely to hear a woman exaggerate the number of guys she's been with. When someone wants to insult a woman, they will likely use her sexuality as a weapon. She's a slut or easy or whatever. If she isn't overtly sexual then she's frigid. People generally talk about women in terms of their sexual attractiveness. Men get this, too, but not close to the same degree.

Personally, I'm grateful that nudity is considered taboo. I'm happy that people are embarrassed by sex and overt sexual expression. If they weren't, I might have had to stay in college and become a lawyer. I think my life would've sucked immensely. I likely wouldn't have met my husband, and while I would have probably had a kid, it would have been with someone else's genetic material. I wouldn't be listening to the unique marvel that is our son, blasting Iron Maiden from his puberty cave. I wouldn't have been a stripper.

Without the guilt and shame our society has about sex and nakedness, I don't think strip clubs would exist at all. You know which people don't really come into the strip club? Nudists. If it was totally normal to see naked humans in an everyday sort of context, I wouldn't have had a job as a nude dancer. If sex was considered just what it is, a normal part of human life, bachelor parties would be terribly boring. Think of poor Ron Jeremy or John Holmes. What would they be doing with their lives? Accountants, maybe?

Without the guilt and shame around sex, I don't think we'd have nearly as much sexual assault and abuse. It is a fact that when you try to repress a natural human drive, it comes out in very unhealthy ways. There would still be people who get off on hurting other people, that is a fucked up psychological problem that would exist either way. I believe there is a good portion of people who would not have acted criminally if they had been allowed to express their sexual urges in a healthy way. There is nothing at all wrong with our bodies or how they function. There is however, a lot of power in keeping people feeling guilty and ignorant about it.

Ignorance Is Not Always Bliss

In some cases, there are definitely things you don't want to know, and once you do, you are not better off. For instance, cats have barbs on their penises. I didn't need to know that, didn't want to know that, and I'm sorry that I now have that information stored in a part of my brain that is readily accessible. Moving on. For the most part, knowledge itself is power. That public service message in the 80s was right: The more you know, the better off you are. People, like Jim, want you to be ignorant and feeling guilty. How else is he going to get you to love and obey him? It was apparently too much effort to just be a nice guy and earn your trust and love.

It's much easier to control people when you control what they are allowed to learn.

The concept of original sin is the act of disobeying God to seek knowledge. Let that sink in. The whole of mankind was doomed to suffer on earth for disobeying a narcissist in order to learn about the world he created. Now every person after the first two must prove their love and obedience to an entity who, although capable, refuses to give any hard evidence for his existence. That pretty much guarantees there will be a lot of people punished after they die. And this entity is supposed to love every one of us, um, OK? He punishes us for our doubt, yet he created us to seek knowledge. Seems like he set his creations up in order to punish them. That would make him a sadist in the truest sense of the word.

If Jim didn't intend for us to suffer, why plant the tree of knowledge at all? He could've just let his little pets live out their lives in paradise. Why test them at all, if not to punish them? The answer must be that he wanted them to know, and then exert his power to feed his own ego when they disobeyed them. If you evaluate it objectively, this is sick and demented behavior.

In our lives we are encouraged to learn about the world. In school, math, science, history, and literature are all subjects we study to get a better sense of the environment in which we will live. That knowledge is intended to help us live better and more productive lives. Would we be better off if we just didn't learn? If we got our information solely through ancient religious texts?

As a species, the more we have learned about our world, the more we have advanced. While there has been some knowledge that has made our world more dangerous, like weapons of mass destruction, for the most part we have made our lives better. Modern medicine, food production, this little computer I'm typing on, have all come from our quest for knowledge. When we as a people failed to question, and simply lived through the stories of other people, advancement stopped. People died of the plague and the ones who dared to question authority were executed. Put in that context, learning is pretty fucking important.

There is an inherent uncomfortableness that comes when we don't have satisfactory answers to profound questions. That's where people tend to want to fill the gap. The easiest way to fill that gap is to simply make shit up. Enter myth and religion. As a way to get a message across, stories are fun and effective. The boy who cried wolf, for example, is a great way to get someone to understand that telling bullshit stories is a good way to get eaten by a wolf. When you make shit up and then threaten someone with death or eternal damnation if they question it, that's when our gap filler becomes dangerous and hurtful.

We are born curious, and in times when our knowledge was severely lacking, myths and tall tales were a good way to explain things. As we learn the truth through observation and the scientific method, we need to drop those primitive explanations. Hanging on to outdated information because you don't like what the actual evidence tells us, is problematic. The scientific method of asking questions and learning through objective evidence can tell us things that do not always coincide with what we thought we knew. And that is a good thing. Being able to question what we think we know and then changing those ideas and opinions based on new evidence is how we move forward and solve problems. Imagine if scientists had rejected the discovery of antibiotics because it didn't mesh with the treatment of bloodletting? There would be a lot fewer people in the world.

Don't tell my husband or my kid, but I'm not always right. That is actually a very good thing because I have been very wrong on some important things. I spent the latter part of my childhood in a small foothill town. Homeopathy was a big thing at the time. I listened to the spiel from the heavily patchouli-ed lady at our local "health" food store and it made sense to me. I bought too much stuff that I couldn't afford and thought I was making great choices. Silly doctors, what do they know? I was so convinced of the effectiveness of these concoctions, that in high school I decided to do a report on it. I studied the peer reviewed scientific studies on homeopathic medicine. Boy, was I ever wrong. I mean really wrong. It was all garbage. My report did not turn out to be what I had intended, but I learned a valuable lesson, and I got an A.

We need to ask questions and seek knowledge about our world, even if it's inconvenient. We are curious for a reason, and that reason is to advance our species. Our brains have evolved to fit that very purpose. Our ability to question and reject silly stories is what got us to where we are, for better or worse. Imagine if we all decided to eat from the tree of knowledge. If we all chose collectively as a united force to look at facts and reject the people who tell us to stop asking. If we took a stand to reject people trying to control us by controlling what we learn, and simply learned for ourselves. What a world we would have.

There is a huge difference between science and the stories of myth and religion when it comes to asking questions and gaining answers. In religion, they try to fit the answers they already have to the questions. In science, they ask the questions and look at the evidence for answers, even if what they find isn't what they hoped for. If a scientist gets an answer he doesn't like, he or she does more research and eventually accepts the results. If religion gets a question they can't answer, they tell you to stop asking questions and just have faith. So basically, just trust Jim, the malignant narcissist.

The tree of knowledge is all around us, and you don't need a talking snake to tell you to eat from it. The more you know and the more comfortable you can be with the fact that you may not always find the answers you want, the happier you will ultimately be. Don't be afraid to seek knowledge. Eat the apple, I double dog dare you.

Chapter 8

Let Your Genitals Be Your Guide

Be True to Yourself

When I started stripping at 18, I knew everything. I mean absolutely everything, with the only exceptions being all the things I didn't know. Which was quite a lot. In 1998, I didn't own a computer or even, brace yourself, a cell phone, as they were still as cumbersome as a dictionary. While the internet existed, websites took around six hours to load, so when it came time to purchase costumes for my new job, I got myself a shiny new Fredrick's of Hollywood mail order catalog. If you didn't know, Fredrick's of Hollywood was a not-so-classy lingerie store that has since succumbed to the vastly superior Victoria's Secret. In 1998, however, they were what I thought of as "the shit."

Perusing through the glossy pages, I picked out several spectacular items, including a strappy vinyl number that looked like something Rob Halford may have sported. I also decided on a glamourous royal blue bra and panty set that was dripping with rhinestones and loops of shiny beads that hung off the bra cups and sides of the panties. It looked gorgeous on the model in the catalog and would obviously look gorgeous on me, too. I also ordered a pair of five-inch black patent high heels. I was most confident in this purchase because my feet are super small, and most stores don't carry adult style shoes in my size.

As was common in times of yore, my package took about six weeks to arrive. When it did, I was so stoked I could hardly contain myself. I opened the box and started to remove the plastic wrapped items. The first thing I tried on was the black vinyl, although by this time, my mentor-of-sorts, Barbie, had gotten her claws into me, and I knew she might not approve of this outfit. Anyway, that quickly became a moot point. After about 30 minutes, I finally got the thing on. A tangle of black plastic and cheap metal chains, I realized quickly that getting out of it in a hurry or gracefully was not going to happen. In fact, after about 15 minutes of struggling, I was worried I may not escape it at all. Houdini himself may not have been able to escape this particular contraption. Not to mention the fact that it looked incredibly stupid on me. Disappointed, I moved on.

Next, the blue thing. It looked beautiful in its cocoon of plastic. I took it out and found it was much easier to put on than the vinyl death trap. Almost too easy. To my utter dismay, I didn't quite fit the cups like the model in the catalog. But the real shocker were the panties. They fit on my hips OK but were really roomy in the crotch. They had a pouch in front that seemed like it was meant to house equipment I didn't have. Then there were all the beaded and rhinestone accoutrements. The entire effect of the outfit looked like I had dissected a chandelier from an eighteenth century brothel and glued it to my mother's bra and a man's thong.

The last hope were the shoes. They were cute enough, but while I was waiting for them to come in the mail, I learned quite a lot about stripper shoes. First off, almost all the girls wore platforms. This is for several practical reasons. The first being that the platform allows for a higher heel without putting the foot at such a steep angle. The higher the platform, the higher the heel; the higher the heel, the better your butt looks. The less steep angle of platforms makes the shoe not only more stable but also much more comfortable for long wear. Only abnormally tall girls wore shoes without platforms, and just to be clear I am not even normally tall.

In addition to being short, I am also rather stubborn. Rather than admit that I didn't in fact know everything and had made an ill-informed rash decision. I wore the damn shoes at work. For about two hours. My feet hurt so bad and the angle of the shoes was so severe that I tottered around like a newborn calf. I threw them away. Reluctantly, I had to admit that I had taught myself a very important lesson. Never buy anything without trying it on.

As stripper costumes go, this wasn't really a big deal - I lost some money, got some blisters, and was a little embarrassed. Had it been a life partner, on the other hand, the consequences may have been much more dire, more expensive, emotionally damaging, and even painful. What may be even more important than trying on clothing is to try on your future spouse. If you make a mistake buying something on a whim, it will be mostly you who has to deal with it. Eventually, you will be able to fix that mistake and hopefully learn from it. Make that kind of mistake in a long-term relationship and the ramifications can impact not only you, but your family, and any potential offspring that results. So why in the world would anyone even consider walking down the aisle without making sure that everything fits?

Most religious teaching involves abstinence before marriage. Frankly, that is far more stupid than buying stripper costumes out of a mail order catalog, which itself is pretty stupid. Marriage is considered a holy union. You are now one within the eyes of the lord. That, in my opinion, is exactly why most marriages fail. Almost all of my most lucrative customers have been in an unhappy marriage. They got married too soon. They were pressured into it by family, friends, girlfriend, or boyfriend, and now they are miserable. Marriage is in its essence a contract, an agreement between two people, but the most important thing is they have to be a good fit. For that, you have to try someone on, maybe a few times. If you try to force it, you could end up with blisters.

Ghostly Ménage à Trois

The only people in your marriage should be living breathing human beings. Seems like common sense. God or any other supernatural force has absolutely nothing to do with your partnership. The idea that you were meant to be with someone, or that there is some kind of purpose outside of your own and your partner's happiness, is crap. Imagine if your nosy neighbor was sitting in the room with you while you're having sex. That would be weird. Why is it any less weird to think that a god is watching you all the time? It's not, because just like your neighbor, God doesn't belong there. Unless he's going to join in, it's ridiculous to think

59

he's somehow involved. In fact, it's kind of fucked up. You didn't marry God, you married a person. I can't imagine a bigger mood killer than the thought of an all-knowing, all-powerful being judging me in my most intimate moments. How would you ever get off? Unless, of course, you're into being watched, then I suppose that might be a good thing.

I truly believe that the most important thing in finding a partner for the long term is sex. For humans, like most animals, sex is one of the most powerful natural drives. In order for our species to survive, we need to make more of us. An urge that strong can compel us to make some tremendously idiotic decisions. Like getting into a marital arrangement that we didn't really want. Like the excitement of a new outfit, a first kiss or touch that blinds us. That jolt of adrenaline can cloud our judgement of reality, and not just the reality of a life decision, but also the reality of our own true desires. It doesn't have to be only the physical excitement of a new partner either, it can be emotional as well. We all want to be loved and desired, and sometimes we are so happy to find someone who is interested in us that we put aside our reservations and doubts in order to feel loved.

As the physical and emotional aspects of our natural instincts can lead us to make brash choices, sometimes there can be a social element leading us, too. The idea that you aren't supposed to have sex until you've found *the one*, is one of them. One of my best customers was someone who stayed a virgin until he married his wife. His wife was also lacking any real sexual experience. Is it any wonder this guy found himself pouring his heart out to a large breasted stripper in an upscale strip club in Reno? Probably not. While running up his credit card, I helped him work through all his feelings about his failing marriage. He loved her, but they were simply not compatible in bed. They both came from religious backgrounds and had gone to pre-marital counseling before being wed. They did all the things they were taught to do, and it failed miraculously.

Now that they were stuck together in a sacred union under God, to leave would be sinful. His wife chalked it all up to God's plan, saying they had to work it out. My customer had a foot fetish and liked brazen redheads, while his wife was a soft-spoken brunette with ticklish feet. These differences are not the kind of thing that can be worked out in counseling. They may have cared for each other, but by following the divine advice and guidance they were given, they doomed themselves to a life of frustration and guilt. Not to mention an astronomical VISA bill, my bad.

All of this could've been avoided with a few sexual trial runs. Just one good romp in the sack and they both would have been able to recognize that they weren't a good sexual match. Thankfully in this case there were no kids involved. God, however, stuck his invisible nose where it didn't belong, and both of these people were now bound together by guilt, shame, and the fear of ostracization by their church and family. Their marriage was more cursed than blessed.

The idea that marriage is somehow blessed by a deity is a great way to keep people in a shitty relationship. If you subscribe to the idea that you are joined by some supernatural force, it can feel like the choice is not entirely yours. It is. If you are in a partnership that you feel is bigger than itself, you can end up stuck there. You wouldn't want to piss off God now, would you? He brought you together and now you need to stay committed.

The idea of a soul mate can have the same consequences. There is no one person out there with whom you are meant to be. In fact, there may be many people with whom you can find an intimate connection. I believe that you need to be connected sexually, intellectually, and emotionally. In that order. To be happy with someone in the long term you need to be connected in all those ways. The most important ingredient to make these connections is to communicate. To be able to effectively communicate your sexual desires, you have to know what they are. To do that, you need experience.

Because of my experience as an adult entertainer, it is very easy for me to compartmentalize the sexual component of my job. For me, sex and love are two completely separate things. Sex carries almost no emotional weight to it. That, it seems, is very different than how most people look at it, but it makes it easy for me to see how relationships go wrong. Sex is sex and love is love. I don't think anyone has to be in love to have great sex. Feel free to argue that point, as my background makes my insight slanted. But, honestly, one of the main issues I have seen in my profession is people being

61

attached emotionally but not sexually. That will almost certainly lead to infidelity or in the case of a lap dance, not quite infidelity, but definitely blue balls.

The key to great long-term sex is to be really open and honest. Open communication is literally the most important aspect of any relationship. I learned this the hard way with my first boyfriend. I was great at giving myself orgasms but had never had one with someone else. My first boyfriend was a virgin when we met. A good portion of my time was spent trying to help him gain confidence. Because I wasn't sure how to direct him to give me an orgasm, and I was trying to boost his ego, I faked it. Seriously, one of the worst mistakes ever. When you fake an orgasm, you pretty much guarantee that you will never have one with that person. All it does is encourage them to keep doing the wrong thing. You are then in the awkward position of having to either confess and hurt their feelings, and in addition look like an asshole, or you just put up with the wrong thing they are innocently doing to your genitals. Forever. God will not help you get off, you have to figure that out yourself.

My husband and I have been married almost twenty years. We both had lots of sex before marriage. God has never been a part of our relationship, ever. How is it that we defy the statistics of divorce? Our marriage is much more like a finance contract than the holy union our non-denominational minister described. I know that sounds lame, but it's true. A marriage is a partnership. Like a contract, there are boundaries that are understood between both people. The one real thing that sets my marriage apart from a finance contract, though, is trust.

Before we ever considered getting married, we fucked a lot. We also talked a lot. We knew we liked hanging out together and had a lot in common. I paid attention to the way he treated other people. My husband has an extreme sense of loyalty, and by examining his other relationships I could safely say that he would also be loyal to me. One of the most baffling things I see in other relationships, usually unhappy ones, is that they will go through each other's phones. Back in the day, I guess, it would be receipts in coat pockets, or sniffing your partner's underwear. I'm grateful we've evolved past those things. If you truly trust your other half there is simply no need to do that. On the few occasions I've browsed through my husband's phone, mostly looking for dirty pictures of myself taken without my knowledge, I've been terribly bored. I've yet to find anything that has made me trust him any less. Trust and communication are absolutely essential.

The other big thing was that we were compatible in bed. If you are going to commit to someone long term, they have to be able to get you off. Full stop. If you don't figure that out ahead of time, you could end up fucked, and not in a good way. Society can put into our heads the idea that to have too much sexual experience before your marriage will make you undesirable to a potential partner. If my husband didn't come to me with the experience he had, I can't imagine that we would be together today. You don't want to be your brain surgeon's first patient, either. You hope he has a lot of experience. Sex partners work exactly the same way. This will sound weird, and maybe it is, but I like hearing about his previous experiences. I feel like a filthy Sherlock Holmes, picking up little clues, that will lead to a more complete understanding of him, and in turn a better sex life.

Sexual experience as well as emotional experience sets you up for a healthy relationship. It can certainly set you up for a bad one, too. The lessons you learn from casual relationships, before you make the plunge, are what will help you stay together in the long run. Another of the most important things you can learn from early relationships is how to have and resolve disagreements. Basically, you need to learn how to disagree. Obviously, not physically fighting, but you will not always agree, and the way those interactions play out will foreshadow the rest of your relationship. For instance, if you or your partner's first reaction to a disagreement is to call names, or otherwise attack, get out. Respect should always be first and foremost. If someone is calling you names or otherwise finding ways to blame or attack you, leave. It's a deal breaker. You can't resolve anything without an underlying basic respect. Being willing and able to see things from their perspective is how you really figure things out, not by attacking.

Don't Be Afraid to Try It On

If you pay attention to what you need physically and emotionally you will be much more likely to find someone you can be with for a long time. But what if you don't want a long-term partner? What if you don't want kids or to be married? Brace yourself...that's OK, too. The *Leave It to Beaver* lifestyle is not for everyone, and that is perfectly fine.

As kids, we are bombarded with images of the perfect family although most of our families don't come anywhere close to that ideal. We are driven by what society says we should be and do. By striving for something we are told is the right way, we can lose sight of our individuality and are thereby more susceptible to the beautiful image we see in the catalog. Giving in to that pressure, and ignoring what you really want, is exactly how you end up with sore feet and stupid outfits, or a bad marriage.

My job has left me desensitized to a certain degree when it comes to all things porn and sex toys, and pretty much anything considered kinky. That becomes all too apparent to me when I visit a sex shop with someone who may not have had one attached to their workplace. For me, browsing through dildos and anal lube is fairly mundane. I am pretty hard to shock these days, but for the non-stripper, it can be a little eye opening, and opening for other orifices as well. If you are limited in your sexual knowledge, I would highly suggest visiting one of these establishments. First maybe by yourself, but also with your partner. You may be uncomfortable at first, but I promise you will learn a lot about yourself and your partner, and probably giggle like school kids in the process.

Done considerately and with express consent, experimenting with things like sex toys, sexual role play – I'm talking about bondage, for example – movies, and costumes can teach you so much about what you like. You may need to start the experimenting on your own, and yes, I mean masturbating. Once you know what tickles your twinkie, you will be better able to direct your partner. You may discover you were into things you never even thought of. The same goes for your partner. You may find new levels of intimacy you didn't think were possible, and that is the kind of bond that can set you up for a successful relationship. It can also rule out a partner who may not be a good long-term fit for you.

Making sure that you fit physically is extremely important also. I had a friend who was quite smitten with a guy and thought that he was the one. When it came time to do the deed, though, it

64

became obvious that it wasn't going to work. What she described when he took his pants down, was like a tree falling, a huge piece of lumber that wasn't going to fit where he wanted it to. That may be awesome to look at and guys may think that having a comically large penis is a good thing, but most of the time it is not. If it is that huge, finding someone who is physically compatible is imperative. Sexual logistics are extremely important and not something you want to find out on your wedding night. Like I said, you don't want to end up with blisters.

Listening to and understanding what your genitals are telling you about yourself can help you determine the right path for your life. The sexual feelings you have can be the biggest clue to living your best and most fulfilling life. Finding the courage to try out a few things will ultimately help you have a fulfilling sex life and partner. Being with the opposite sex may not be for you. You might not even be the gender everyone thought you were born as. Maybe you want to be in an open relationship, or no relationship at all. Or what you really want is to be a stay at home parent and homemaker. For me, by paying attention to my desires, I found balance. I love baking cookies, reading *Better Homes and Gardens*, and taking my clothes off in public. Balance. By understanding myself, I was able to communicate those things and find someone who loves and accepts me. June Cleaver by day and brazen hussy by night happens to be exactly what my husband wanted, also. If I had ignored my exhibitionist tendencies, the life he and I have would not have been possible.

The pressure we feel to be and have what others want for us can be overwhelming. The fear of rejection can drive us to do things we don't otherwise want, like getting married. It takes a lot of courage to decide what you really want for own life, especially when you know you will face criticism. Sometimes that means letting go of the traditions or ideals we have grown up with. Without proper support, letting go of those can seem impossible. In some cases, the fear of rejection can be deadly.

When I was a sophomore in high school, there was an especially annoying boy in my typing class. He sat in front of me, and any chance he got he would turn around and say something sexual. Not directed toward me, but he would take any chance he got to talk about sex with girls. How hot someone was, how much he wanted to fuck someone. That he was particularly vulgar was not really anything that stood out to me, we were teenagers after all. One day I learned he had hung himself. In the note he left, he revealed that he was gay. He was acutely aware that he would never be what his family wanted him to be. Instead of accepting himself and the life he could have had, he chose to die. I will never forget him. I wish I could have given him a hug and told him that gay is awesome. I feel pain, regret, and anger for his lost life. Even twenty-five years later, I cry when I think of what his fear of rejection led him to do. I probably don't have to tell you that he came from a very religious family. Although he was taught to fear God, what he feared most was being rejected by the people he loved.

What happened to that boy is utterly unacceptable. I'm sorry to end a chapter with such a disturbing story, but it reminds us of an important lesson. We need to be able to accept ourselves first. If you are blinded by fear, religion, or any ideas that go against who you are inside, life will be harder for you. The reality is that denying who you are and what you really want is ultimately the wrong thing to do. Unless what you want is to hurt people, the best thing you can do for yourself and the other people around you is to be true to yourself.

Chapter 9

Praying for Control

Rethink Your Mental Talking

Trapped in a lap dance booth and desperately trying to ignore the building pressure in my belly, I close my eyes to say a quiet little prayer in my mind. The song which is supposed to be limited to three and a half or four minutes at the most, feels like it will never end. I'm slowly moving in the lap of a gentleman who is completely enthralled with my performance. For the sake of aesthetics, I am doing everything I can to keep my stomach muscles tight, hoping I don't give away my current discomfort. I'm terrified that if I relax my abdomen, I will reveal the secret that I am hiding. I have to pee. Badly. What or who will bring an end to this nightmare?

I keep my eyes closed in hopes that if I focus on the wish I'm repeating in my head, the endless song will end. This continuous loop of begging is running through my mind that I hope will be heard. My relentless mental begging is in part distracting me from the horror of the lap dance I'm performing. Finally, I hear the DJ start to talk into the mic, indicating that finally this song is over. My prayer has been answered. I express my relief and gratitude in another silent plea. My gratitude is short lived, however, as the man underneath me tells me he wants another song. Crap. It's a slow night, close to the end of the month, and there just aren't very many other potential customers, so I continue dancing.

I also continue my silent wishes. They seemed to be answered the first time, so why not keep doing it? There are plenty of girls on the stage list, and it seems at least possible that the DJ might keep the songs to the minimum time in order to move through the list faster. I hope and wish once again that my silent pleas will be heard, and the songs will be kept short. This time my prayer doesn't work. I count the choruses in the song and can tell it's going over the time. I suspect that my DJ has left the booth for a smoke, oblivious to my suffering. Or maybe he is aware of my plight and is trying to teach me a lesson? Patience, tolerance, endurance? Who am I to question the guy in charge? He is the man in the booth, and I have no choice but to trust his judgement. I am once again wishing that the DJ will grant me mercy in my time of need.

When I pray to the strip club DJ, it would appear that he answers my prayers about fifty percent of the time. Why he chooses this ratio, I do not fully grasp. When I am dancing in the lap of someone who is less than pleasant, or I am experiencing physical discomfort, my beloved DJ seems to respond to my silent communications at his own whim. Sometimes he is gracious and grants a reprieve, while other times he seems to want to prolong my discomfort. Still, if I am able to accrue a significant profit, I give him a generous tip. Even if I don't fully understand his reasons or agenda, I still make sure I give him his proper due in hopes that he will show me mercy the next time. I make sure he knows that I am grateful.

As the guy in charge of the music, a strip club DJ is one of the most powerful members of the staff. He controls when you go on stage, what music you can play, and probably the most important thing for an aging stripper, the stage lights. There is no one who can make you more miserable and impact your money as much as the DJ. You could even go as far as to say he is very nearly deified in his position. Keeping your DJ happy is paramount to your success as a stripper.

If one out of every two times I say a prayer to my DJ he gives me what I prayed for, would that be considered effective? Could we confidently conclude that praying actually succeeds at that ratio? In the case of the strip club DJ, I think we can say the answer is no. I am simply making myself feel just a little better by fooling myself into thinking I can gain some semblance of control of the situation. Praying makes me feel like I am doing something when I really can't do anything. Of course, in the case of an unfortunate lap dance, I always have a choice. I can quit anytime I want to, but when money is at stake, it doesn't always feel like a choice. If my financial motives are strong enough, and the situation is not dangerous, I won't quit. What I can do instead is pretend that I have some control by *praying* to the DJ. When it feels like it works, I'm thrilled. When it doesn't, I chalk it up to just part of being a stripper. When my DJ fails to grant my prayer, I never blame him. When it feels like he does hear me, I sing his praises.

Efficacy of Prayer

There is much debate on the effectiveness of prayer. The most notable study of the efficacy of prayer was done on heart surgery patients. There were two groups of patients with similar conditions and treatments. One group was told of prayers being said for their recovery, while the other group had no group praying for them. The group that had prayers said for them felt slightly better than the non-prayer group. Compelling? Not quite. After examining the results, it was determined that the prayer group's slightly better results had more to do with positive thinking than divine intervention. They thought they were feeling better, but medically the results were about the same as the non-prayer group. More like a watered-down placebo effect than a miraculous recovery.

Some would say if it helps even a little, why not pray? Unless you are counting on it, I think prayer can be a positive thing. Anything that makes you feel better during a tough time is a positive thing and can seem to help facilitate healing. When and if prayer alone replaces medical treatment, that is a problem and can be deadly. Unfortunately, it is usually children who are the casualties of their parents' misplaced faith in prayer. There are some laws that seek to prevent this kind of neglect, but they are not always effective. Not getting medical treatment for a sick child is abuse, pure and simple. However, as a parent of a kid who oddly prefers the dentist to going to school, I can understand that figuring out when to seek medical treatment can get a little tricky. Sometimes you don't go. Most of the time I have erred on the side of caution, even though I've been duped before. I have shelled out an unnecessary copay and will most likely do it again, so I understand reasonable reluctance, but not abandoning all medical help when needed.

69

Most of the credit that goes to prayer when it comes to medical circumstances can be explained simply by positive thinking, if not by the medical help itself, of course. Your frame of mind and mental resilience will help you feel better. That's why they allow comfort animals in the hospital, that little boost of positivity makes a big difference. When I feel like crap and my toothless old cat comes and sits next to me, I feel better. I know that it's entirely possible that he is simply waiting for me to die so he can eat my eyeballs, but I choose to think he loves me. The affection I may or may not be getting from my bag of fur and bones brings me comfort. Prayer can3 function just like that.

Just as I choose to get comfort from my dilapidated cat, some people choose to get comfort from praying. That comfort feels as real as the comfort I get from my cat, but neither the prayer nor the cat actually has any real effect on the physical condition. The way the human mind reacts to that kind of comfort is what helps. The calming effect that starts in your brain helps to relax the body and promotes a better emotional state. If you don't want to pray and don't like animals, meditation can produce the same results.

Meditation is not just for your fruity old auntie, who took too much LSD and changed her name to Starfire Moonbeam. The simple act of calming your mind and breathing deeply has almost exactly the same effect as prayer. The real difference between meditation and prayer, the former is taking control of your own mind, while the latter is asking someone or something else to control your situation. The connection between your mind and your physical body is real and powerful. Have you ever gone to the doctor with some strange symptoms only to be told to reduce your stress? Stress in all its forms has a massively negative effect on the body. Just as meditation, a positive mindset, and support have a positive effect, stress does the opposite.

When you meditate, exercise, or otherwise pay attention to your mental state, you will gain a better understanding of yourself and whatever issue you are going through at the time. When you take a break from the endless stream of anxiety-provoking thoughts, you are actively taking control. By choosing to take care of yourself in this way, you can approach your problems, medical or otherwise, with a more objective perspective. That will go a long way toward evaluating and choosing the right solution. By actively working to solve your problems in the real world, whether successful or not, you are taking control.

Who's Listening?

When I was a little kid saying my prayers at night like I was supposed to, I had a hard time thinking anyone was really listening. To not believe was heresy, punishable by an eternity in a lake of fire, so I tried my damnedest to believe someone was listening. Even as a little kid, I had a hard time thinking I wasn't just talking to myself. My family seemed to miss the irony, though, of telling me that imaginary friends weren't real and that talking to myself was weird. I learned early on that pointing out this hypocrisy never ended well, so I decided to let it go.

When I was having trouble or wanted something, I was told to pray. I was also told that God had a plan and would only grant a prayer if it was meant to be. This was stated in the bible and taught in Sunday school. Only once did I have the balls to ask what the point was of asking God for things when he had already made up his mind. I was sent to the corner for a time out. I was told that my *smart mouth* was not appreciated. Had I been able to completely explain my reasoning, I would have pointed out the fact that if I asked for something at the grocery store, and my mom had already told me that she wasn't going to buy anything extra, begging was futile. In fact, if I kept asking, it would usually only serve to piss off my mom and lessen my chances of getting anything in the future.

Why do we bother to ask God to change his mind? Granted, my mom would give in occasionally, which is the only reason I continued to bug her. When we pray, are we trying to get God to change his mind? Maybe instead of asking politely in our heads, we should scream and cry loudly in public in hopes that he will give in to us to stop his own public embarrassment. Is God really prone to that kind of manipulation? Does he take pleasure in our pleas, knowing he is going to do what he wants anyway? Like a bully holding your head over the toilet, he wants you to think that if you cry loud enough, he won't actually dunk your head in. You both know he's definitely going to dunk your head in the toilet because, well, he's a bully.

The very act of praying to a god in hopes that you will change his mind, is revealing to that god that you doubt his intentions. If you had faith in whatever plan you think God has for you and that he has your best interest at heart, why don't you just roll with it? If your faith is that unshakeable, wouldn't you feel comfortable in the fact that whatever he has planned is just fine? The logic simply doesn't pan out here. If you are to give total control to God and his plan, then praying is moot. If you choose to have faith, is there any point in praying at all?

One thing that seems to go unsaid, is when prayers are not answered, God never bears the blame. It may be easy to see this as part of a divine plan if you, say, fail your driver's test the first time, but what about unanswered prayers about the really big stuff? Starving or abused kids for instance. How many kids who were raised to believe in prayer have prayed for food or for abuse to stop? What does that do to their emotional well-being to think their prayers are being ignored? Sure, maybe you didn't get the new toy you prayed for, that seems fair enough, but what if you're starving? Somehow, we are supposed to have faith that God's plan is ultimately good, even if it means tremendous suffering now.

I have noticed posts on various platforms citing a miracle that a cross survived some natural disaster while humans and property are devastated. This is usually taken as a sign that God is there and providing hope, totally ignoring the fact that people are dead, and lives are ruined. God gets all the credit and none of the blame. If you're part of a soccer game, that would be like winning a trophy because you managed to keep your pants on, even though you lost the game. Keeping your pants on is simply not worthy of a prize. If God chose to spare a symbol of his worship while destroying a thousand homes, he doesn't deserve praise.

If it seems like I am a little hostile to the idea of prayer, the truth is I am. Since the age of reason, I have considered myself a non-believer, well before I even knew of the word atheist. I was simply not able to logically believe in a benevolent being who controlled life on earth. To say that I didn't try to believe would be disingenuous. I tried a lot. I just kept failing. The last time I really tried to have faith in prayers to a god, it left me very angry and feeling kind of stupid.

Shortly after my wedding, my two-year-old nephew was diagnosed with a very aggressive cancer. For six years we went through the ups and downs of various treatments. Complicating the situation was the tumultuous situation between my brother and his ex-wife, which left me and the majority of my side of the family alienated from this child. There was very literally nothing I could do to help. So, like everyone else in my family, I prayed. I figured, if I put all my good intentions into it and really believed, maybe I could make it better. In the end, neither prayer nor medical treatments helped. He passed at age 8, but not before losing his hair and teeth. It was really one of the most awful things imaginable. I was left feeling angry and helpless. That experience left me with not so much of a chip on my shoulder in terms of the efficacy of prayer, but a huge fucking boulder. So, I'm willing to admit that I'm a little biased on the subject.

When we pray, we are hoping to influence something to intervene and help us. Just like when I felt like I was stuck in an unending lap dance, I prayed because it felt like I was doing something. There was no way my DJ was hearing my thoughts, but it felt better to give my mind something to cling to, rather than focus on my painfully full bladder. Praying gives you something to do when you feel helpless. Even if praying doesn't have any physical effects in the real world, if you really believe it will help then it can have real benefits. While I am personally jaded regarding prayer, I can't deny the real comfort it offers to those who believe it is helping. Whether praying to a god or the universe or even the strip club DJ, the simple act of directing your thoughts in a positive way can help and provide some comfort.

One of my favorite quotes comes from a lady who was dubbed the "most hated woman in America". That seems a little harsh if you ask me, but her name was Madalyn Murray O'Hair. She said, "Two hands working can do more than a thousand clasped in prayer." When I first heard this quote, I was immediately amazed and impressed that someone had the courage to speak this out loud. Something which, despite my apparent smart mouth, even I would've been afraid to say. It couldn't be truer, however. When we are presented with a difficult situation and feel helpless, prayer offers a way to give us something to do. The problem with hoping and praying for something is that the only thing we are helping is ourselves.

When bad things happen, my first reaction is to see if there is any real thing I can do to help. Can I send money, donate blood or other needed items, volunteer, or maybe just offer some words of comfort and a shoulder to cry on? There are some times, for sure, when there is really nothing you can do. In that case, you may just need to accept that fact and move on.

The only real way to help is to look outside your own mind and see where you are able to make things better. It may be nice to think that your thoughts are actually having an impact outside of yourself, but they aren't. I have found that most of the time there are many things you can do to help in a shitty situation. Very recently, there was a devastating fire in Northern California that very literally wiped out an entire town. When it happened, there were calls for monetary donations, and I simply didn't have any cash to spare. Having known someone from the area, I asked what specifically was needed. I got a surprising list, that consisted mostly of common household items, such as toys, blankets, jackets, pet food and things like that. My family and I went through every drawer and closet and found that we had much to give. We were able to donate three large bags of almost new items that would go directly to those in need. We saw where we could do good and took action.

When faced with a personal situation where it seems like your only option is to pray, I would challenge you to think differently about it. Pray if it helps you but see if there is anything you can do about it that helps someone else. You can look to see how other people handled a similar problem. Maybe consult a professional or search the internet for more information. I have found that when I think the problem is unsolvable, I am usually wrong. It can be easy to be blinded to solutions when you're upset. Sometimes a deep breath, long walk, or pleasant workout can help clear your mind and approach a problem from a different angle. Finding a sympathetic friend is also a good idea.

Sometimes there is simply nothing you can do. In that case, acceptance is your only option. There are times when things just suck and that's it. We can't always control the problems we are faced with, but looking for solutions or accepting what we can't control is always better than just wishing it were different. While it is hard to simply accept that a situation is beyond our control, a good thing to keep in mind is that every situation is only temporary. Every song, no matter how endless it may seem at the time, will end.

Chapter 10

Finding Your Own Heaven

Live As If Now Is All You Get

"Did it hurt?" he asks. I know what's coming next, but I have to play the game. "Did what hurt?" I ask. "When you fell from heaven," he says with a stupid grin, "You must be an angel." I smile back and ask if he wants another song. I already know he does, but I'm trying to be polite. If I'm an angel, I might be closer to Lucifer, than an ethereal being with wings and a harp. With fake eyelashes glued to my face, a ton of makeup, dark lighting, and the high probability that this dude has been drinking, I suppose I could look like an angel. I think if you try hard enough, the velour-covered booth might even seem just a little like heaven. OK, maybe not.

For a little while at least, this guy feels like he's in heaven. He hasn't figured out yet that this is simply an illusion created for his entertainment. He might not ever figure it out, and that is really OK. He let me know that he had a long rough day, and I was showing him just a little bit of heaven to help him forget about it. It might seem like a bit of a stretch, but for some people, time away from their problems, in a badly upholstered semi-private booth can be heaven. That I look like an angel may be more of an indication that this guy needs a visit to the eye doctor than a compliment, but I'll take it.

Heaven for me was on a beach on the Hawaiian island of Kauai. Standing under a small stream of fresh water trickling down from a cliff through emerald vines and purple flowers, I was struck by the utter beauty of it all. Having just come from a long session of playing in the waves, I was enjoying the fact that this beach had access to both the ocean and freshwater. As I was rinsing the salt from my hair I was overwhelmed by the sheer awesomeness of nature. I looked up into the lush greenery from where the water was coming and noticed a brightly colored spider the size of a moving van. If I had seen the same spider in a different setting, I think I would have bolted. Where I was just then, though, I was able to continue enjoying the moment, without screaming in terror. In fact, the spider and I seemed to have come to a silent understanding. It decided to stay where it was while I chose to slowly move a little farther down the way. The serenity I was surrounded by appeared to have calmed my fight or flight response. Heaven.

There are many concepts of heaven or the afterlife. The idea that after we are done in this life there is an eternal paradise waiting for us, provided we haven't been too much of an asshole, is prevalent in many cultures. The guys that flew a plane into the twin towers in New York were expecting to be rewarded with 72 virgins. Kind of makes you wonder what the 72 virgins thought about being someone's reward in the afterlife. Was that a reward or punishment for them? But I digress. I think the one thing that ties all these ideas together is the fear of death. The fear of not knowing what's going to happen when we die. An unpleasant thought is made just a little easier by the concept of heaven.

We know that energy doesn't die, it just basically changes form. We know that there is a part of us that is energy. We are pretty sure that consciousness probably doesn't survive outside of our skulls. Does the part of us that thinks and has self-awareness go beyond our physical beings? Not trying to be a Debbie Downer here, but as far as we know, it doesn't. Granted, there is a lot about consciousness that we simply don't understand. One of the best things about science is that it is always looking for answers, and that if it finds contradictory evidence of something, it changes its position. There are scientists right now looking for evidence of a soul, although they have yet to find it. So far, there has not been any conclusive proof that says there is. A majority of physicists think that we simply go back to be the stardust we came from. A life after this one is far from guaranteed, and that should make the life we know we have that much more important. Accepting that we are likely to simply end, rather than continue after our bodies are gone, can be rough, but also liberating. While you may lose the comfort of thinking you will get to live on after death, you gain an understanding of how profoundly important life can be now. Most of the time, even the shitty parts are better than nothing at all.

Live Now

Looking at it objectively, we know we can't count on an afterlife. While it seems like that is a bummer, is it really? If all we know we have for certain is this moment, doesn't that make this moment seem that much more special? When I was a little kid, and I knew I was going to spend the day at Disneyland, I knew all I had for sure was that one day. Maybe I would go back, but the only thing I was certain of was that I was there right then. I was going to make the best of it. For that one day, I was going to have the best possible time. I was going to meet Goofy, ride all the rides I was tall enough for (not many), and maybe get my big brother to buy me one of those huge rainbow lollipops that I would lick twice and throw away. If there was a chance I would never come back to this magical place, then I was going to cherish every moment I had. As it turned out, because we lived in Southern California, I would go to Disneyland far more times than any kid should. But I wouldn't know that until I was a lot older.

If we focus too much on what we can't know, we lose sight of what we have right now. For the first two days I was in Kauai, I kept my phone with me. I was taking pictures and checking Facebook, until it hit me. I was wasting my trip. Once I left my phone in the rental car, my vacation took on a whole new meaning. Likes on my sunset pictures be damned. I took the time to look around, to create memories that Facebook would never know. I relished every second I had there, not even the horrific sight of what could've been (probably wasn't) a deadly spider could have spoiled my time. There were a few naysayers who criticized the expense of the trip, but frankly, if it meant eating ramen noodles for a year, I would've spent the money anyway. The memories I have and will hopefully have for the rest of my life were totally worth it.

Obviously, we need to think about tomorrow, too. If you want to avoid retirement in a cardboard box under a freeway overpass, then you must plan ahead. It is quite possible to savor the moment in the moment while also making sure you'll be able to afford food in the future. It takes some thought, but it is totally doable. Unless you happen to be independently wealthy, smart budgeting is how you can ensure that you make the most of what you have now, while not eating dog food when you're eighty. In my case, once a year, my husband and I set out our priorities. House repairs, upcoming medical expenses, and hopefully a little retirement savings, and then we discuss the fun part. In our yearly budget goals, we always include a family trip or activity. While the other things are very important, we put a high value on the time we spend together. Looking at our son's emerging mustache, we are acutely aware that our time with him as a child is coming to an end. That makes us extremely motivated to experience what we can with him, before he moves out and forgets to call.

One of the biggest traps I see people fall into when it comes to prioritizing their lives, is the pervasive thought of an afterlife. I know one person in particular who loathes to spend any extra money on anything they consider frivolous. Now, their house is nearly paid off, they have a respectable retirement account, and will most definitely retire comfortably, assuming they make it that far. That sounds horribly cynical, but the reality is, for most people death comes as a surprise. There are so many things that could go wrong at any moment, and while a certain amount of planning is obviously prudent, restricting any and all fun now is a little excessive in my opinion.

When I asked this person why they felt so strongly about depriving themselves of so many of the things they would like to have now, the answer I got was, "Because I'll have everything I want in Heaven." So, let me get this straight. You are holding off on buying the $200 car stereo you really want, and denying yourself the trip to Alaska you've been dreaming of, despite the fact that you can comfortably afford it, because you're waiting to die? This person is totally capable of reaching their financial retirement goals, while enjoying the things they want, but is choosing to wait for heaven to be happy. When I made the choice to point out that it's possible, even likely, that we return to stardust, I was greeted with a look that made my skin crawl. That there could be no heaven was a concept that simply didn't register with this person.

This same person loves to point out how wasteful are the trips and other things I choose to spend my money on in order to obtain pleasure. The naked resentment and bitterness that bleeds into these conversations are disheartening, to say the least. I can't help but find it incredibly sad to be counting on an afterlife to be happy. Ironically, this person feels that because I choose to look for things to enjoy now, that I will ultimately suffer for an eternity. Two vastly different perspectives on life. One is to suffer now and to live forever on a cloud, hopefully. The other is to enjoy life while it's here while implementing a respectable plan for the future. While both of us pity each other, one of us is at least having a good time, and without an ugly sense of animosity toward others who choose to be happy.

While money is certainly helpful, it isn't totally necessary to savor your life now. There are plenty of ways to enjoy your life on earth right now. Simply taking a walk and taking the time to look at the beauty around you is something you can do every day. Reading a book, finding a good movie, enjoying an ice cream cone, laughing with friends, taking the time to find pleasure in the things you like to do is all you need. Every single day you can find something heavenly to find pleasure in.

Mom Is Not in Heaven

I was thirty-four when I lost my mom. Those are hard words to write even now, over five years later. The truth is, I feel cheated. I feel cheated out of time I feel I should have had with her, and also the time my son should've had with her. My mom was almost forty when she had me, so generally speaking she was older than most moms of kids my age. The fact that I was likely going to have less time with her than most people doesn't make it any easier. I'm still angry. I am aware that my anger is largely unjustified, but it's still there. My mother went in for what was supposed to be a fairly straightforward surgery. After a week in medically induced unconsciousness, she never recovered. There is no one to be angry at, it just happened.

I held the hand of the priest along with my siblings as he performed the last rites over our mother. Despite my unbelief in God or an afterlife, I was still able to draw some comfort from this ritual. Partly because I knew that this was what my mom wanted, but also because I knew that my family was comforted by it. After the priest left, only my youngest brother and I stayed. I had wrongly assumed that once someone was removed from life support that it would be over fairly quickly. Twelve hours and several pots of thick coffee later, the heart monitor started to speed up, an indication that her heart was going to stop. I held on to one hand, while my brother had the other, until I started to see the heart rate normalize. My brother had to tell me that it was no longer registering our mother's heartbeat, but because I was holding on so tight, it was actually registering my own heartbeat. She was gone. At that moment I wanted nothing more than to be gone with her.

My mother was my biggest supporter, my closest confidant, and easily my best friend. When I told her to stop chasing my son around her house with a bottle of holy water in a futile attempt at baptizing him, she was disappointed, but respectful. I finally succeeded by asking her if she really thought God would send him to hell because I chose to not put some stale water on him. She relented, and said, "Well, I guess not." Of all the people I confessed my non-belief to, she was the kindest. She said she knew that the bible stories were fiction, but she still wanted to believe in God. She never told me I would go to hell or not get to heaven. She said I was a good person, and that was all that mattered. Her indoctrination into religion was strong, but not strong enough to override her sense of love and empathy.

My mom held on to the belief that she would see her parents in heaven. Just before she lost consciousness for the last time, I asked her one last favor. I asked her to fight, she nodded her head and closed her eyes. That was our final communication. I don't know how much of her own will had to do with her final passing, but part of me still wonders if she let go thinking that her mom and dad were waiting for her. That she felt like she could go and see me and my brothers and sisters in an afterlife. Would she, if she could have, fought harder to stay if she thought it was the real end? This thought haunts me.

For about a week, I walked around in a dazed stupor. I could barely eat, I got down to the weight I was in eighth grade. The grief was unrelenting. Family and friends talked about her being in a better place and not in pain anymore. A harpist in real life, they laughed about her getting her heavenly harp with her wings. For a time, I tried to believe these ideas, but ultimately, I was unsuccessful. I simply couldn't do it and please understand that I was in so much pain I really did try. I did not, however, let anyone know that I didn't share their visions of heaven. I was almost jealous of the relief they felt in that belief, but I thought it would be cruel to tell them what I really thought.

Over the next few weeks, as the fog of grief began to fade slightly, I examined my thoughts about mortality. While my initial reaction was to want to go with her, I started to think about what she would've wanted for me. It didn't take very long before I was able to realize she would've wanted me to live my life. I was in the process of writing my first book, and because she was one of my biggest cheerleaders, I knew I would have to finish it. She loved my son and would've wanted him to thrive. My husband loved my mother deeply and also understood that the best way to honor her would be to live the best lives we could. I had come to a crossroads at that point. I could crawl under my bed and give in to my almost debilitating grief, or I could live on. I chose to live on.

The hole she had left in my life was still there, however, and without the idea of an afterlife, I had to figure out how to come to grips with that. At first, there was her stuff. Her piano, her sunhat, jewelry, and the other physical things she left behind. Because my mother was oddly frugal, she would collect the free items from her hospital stays; shampoo, soap, and those awful little socks with the rubber on the bottom. I felt unable to let them go. Over the years, she had liked to send care packages in the mail with various things she thought we might like. On one occasion, she had accidentally included denture cleaning tablets in one of the boxes. After she died, I found them, laughed, but kept them. I couldn't let go of the idea that to throw those things away, would be to lose her all over again.

While I grew accustomed to the sadness I felt every day, I finally got to a point where I could talk or think about her without bursting into tears. I've heard people say that grief gets easier. They're fucking wrong. It does not. You build a kind of tolerance to it. It still hurts, you are just able to control the outward reactions to it. For me it has not diminished. The thought of her just not existing anymore was unbearable. Then one day it changed. Not the pain, the way I thought about her.

My husband and son were talking about my mom and laughing at one of the numerous corny jokes she used to tell. A weird thing happened. It was like she was still there. I had a sense of her in the room. I know obviously that she wasn't, but something made me feel like she could've been. I let it go at the time, but that feeling would come again.

The next time I would sense my mom, I was in the dressing room of a department store. I had just gotten my boobs done and was trying on dresses. I have a very small waist and ample hips, and with my newly enhanced breasts I had gotten stuck in a dress I was trying on. I was unable to get it over my hips or my boobs. I was trapped. I started to laugh because, frankly, I didn't know what to do. Then I caught sight of my ass in the mirror and realized that it was not my ass at all. It was Mom's ass. She had a figure much like my own, with a tiny waist and wide hips that had facilitated myself and five siblings. I knew then that she was still there. At least the part of her that was in me. If I wanted to see my mom, all I had to do was look at my own butt. I laughed out loud when I understood how hilarious she would have thought this whole debacle was. Me, stuck in an expensive dress, and finding comfort in the big butt she gave me. I found my mom.

After that, I saw her everywhere. My eyes, my nose, the silly jokes we remembered. I saw her in my son, my brothers, and my sister's ass. The healing started then, the real healing. I was able to dump the awful bottles of hospital shampoo, and the itchy socks. I admit that I held on to the denture tablets if only because it was so funny, and because she loved to torture me by removing her teeth at the worst possible times. I realized that she had left so much of herself behind that even if I couldn't see or talk to her anymore, she was still there if I wanted to see her. I didn't need to think of her as an angel in heaven. She was still here on earth.

I am very fortunate that my mom was a musician who had recorded several albums, one of which contains her voice. At times when I need her the most, I can hear her. I can also share her with other people. Even in death, she is still bringing joy to people she hasn't even met. While the date of her death is ingrained in my mind, I choose to celebrate her birthday. I try to do something special in her honor to remember her and help to keep her memory alive, even if her body is not.

Life is not always flowers and sausages. Life sucks sometimes, but it's the only one we've got. When we are faced with shitty situations like the death of a loved one, the things we don't know about our world can be hard to face. That is why the idea of an afterlife exists at all. It exists because death is scary and loss hurts, and to not know what happens when we die is hard to deal with. So as humans, we made up an idea to make us feel better, but if you aren't able to believe in it, it really doesn't help much. I hope more than anything that I am wrong. I hope that my mom was able to be with her parents again, and that I would be able to see my mom again. There is just nothing to back up that hope. What I can do is live a life she would be proud of and to honor her memory where I can. While I don't really think my mom is in heaven, I do know that at least part of her is still with me, even if I have to look at my own ass to see it.

On that island in the middle of the pacific, I had an epiphany. I discovered that life is right now. It's not tomorrow, it's not yesterday, it's right now. The future isn't here yet and is not guaranteed. The past is gone. Right now is the only time we have. Expose yourself to what is around you right now. Ponder how you can take your own risks. Challenge your own thinking about death. Let go of guilt and shame, and wishful thinking when it comes to loved ones we've lost. We haven't lost their love in our lives, and being happy now is the best way to honor them.

Chapter 11

Letting Go of Hell

Doing Good Feels Good

The feeling of dread that has been building all morning has morphed into a full-blown panic. A wave of nausea threatens to expel the Captain Crunch you ate for breakfast. You don't understand why this is happening. You're not perfect for sure, but what could you have done to deserve this punishment? You open the car door and look one last time at your loving creator who has sent you here for your own good. The too warm air hits you in the face and reminds you of the huge pimple that has formed on your nose. Reluctantly, you step out onto the concrete and shut the door behind you. As you watch the vehicle of salvation drive away, you are acutely aware of the eternity that stretches out before you.

A crowd of sinister looking demons immediately engulfs you. There are a few in the crowd of snickering faces who appear to be as confused and terrified as you are, but most of them have very obvious evil intentions. You look down at the piece of paper that is supposed to tell you where you should go, but the words suddenly become meaningless gibberish. Your fear and panic reach its crescendo as you spot Satan herself. Her beautiful dark hair hides an intense malice. Her only purpose in this realm is to cause you as much pain and humiliation as possible. In a futile attempt to avoid her attention, you dash quickly to the nearest building, but it's too late.

Satan not only sees you, but the little friend hitching a ride on your nose. "Hey freckleface, looks like you're trying to grow a second nose," she spits. Her minions erupt into unwarranted laughter. The large pimple almost disappears as the rest of your face turns the same shade of red. As you think this couldn't get any worse, the boy you've had a crush on for the last two years is standing only a few feet away. Not only has he witnessed this exchange, but also seems to be staring directly at the throbbing zit in the middle of your face.

Satan sees him also and seizes this new torture opportunity to point out your well-intended but ultimately hideous new hairdo. Last week, you went to your mother's hair stylist with the idea that you could make yourself look slightly less awkward, but you are now being punished for your pride and vanity. The spiral perm should've made you look like Jessie Spano from Saved by the Bell. What happened instead was a frizzy ball of fluff. In a futile attempt to mitigate the damage, you cut it into a short bob creating a mushroom effect. Unfortunately, mushroom head is not what they will call you. Satan will now refer to you as "Penis Head," and so will the rest of the demons she controls.

Eventually, you make it to the dark corner of this place where you've been assigned. Hoping maybe there will be someone or something to ease your suffering. But in this place all hope is lost. You have been sent here to suffer and that is exactly what will happen. There is no joy or hope, only despair in this wasteland. The hot and dry atmosphere only adds to your discomfort as it feels like fall is still lifetimes away. All of your good intentions have led you to this place of endless torment. You have been sentenced to hell, otherwise known as the 7th grade.

Hell Is for Children

As a child I was taught that hell was where really bad people went after they died. Hell was the reason you didn't do bad things. Be good or you'll go to hell. Cartoons, church, and movies all illustrated this concept. By the time I reached middle school, I no longer thought this was a viable idea. Middle school, for me, was hell. Even though it lacked the burning lake of fire depicted in church, it definitely contained its share of devils, demons, and all-around bad people. I might seem a little overly dramatic here, but for me the fear and anxiety I felt about school was extreme. I felt like I couldn't go a whole day without some unprovoked humiliation.

The idea of a crimson colored dude with a pitchfork seemed like a joke compared to the cruelty of the pre-teen girls who lurked in every hallway of my middle school. Because I was born a skeptic, I had a hard time believing that the idea of hell was anything but fear-based motivation to get kids to behave. It seemed to me like the majority of people also thought it was bullshit. The girl I refer to as "Satan" certainly didn't seem afraid of burning for all eternity. She was not afraid of God's wrath when she was breaking down the door to the bathroom stall I was changing in for PE. It was pretty obvious to me that hell was nothing but an idle threat. If hell is real, then the real Satan will meet his match when my bully finally makes it there.

When it became apparent to me that the fear of going to hell didn't stop a lot of people from being assholes, I decided it was not real. Simple logic would suggest that if everyone believed that hell was real, then everyone would be good. After all, who wants to go to hell? In church I had learned that one could be forgiven for their sins or bad deeds and avoid hell, but what if you died before you had a chance to confess? Hell, then, is just a place for people who didn't have a chance to say they were sorry. Why bother doing the right thing at all if you can simply be forgiven afterward and avoid the punishment? Like a poorly made sweater, pull just one tiny thread of logic and the whole thing comes apart.

The other thing that seemed illogical to me about the idea of hell was that, if you are simply being good to avoid punishment, are you really a good person? If I decide not to steal something I really want, not because I think that it is a fucked-up thing to do, but because I'm afraid of being caught, am I really a good person? Or am I just a thief who is afraid of punishment? Put that way, the idea of hell and the devil functions more like a security guard than a guide to morality. Hell, to me, was nothing more than a scary story that was presented deliberately to get kids to be good. The devil was just the antithesis to Santa Claus. Be good, get presents; be bad, go to hell. Hell seemed designed specifically for children.

Hell used as a deterrent only works if you really believe in it. Teaching children they must be good or they will be punished forever, in my humble opinion, is wrong. Kids, by their very nature, look up to adults, especially parents. They look to grown-ups to explain this world that they've been born into. It may seem like a good way to teach morality, but is it really? Adults shelter kids from scary movies and sex, but somehow, it's OK to tell them that the god that made them will torture them forever if they don't follow his rules? The graphic description of hell that comes from stories, the bible, and even children's cartoons are not only terrifying, but seem inappropriate for children in general.

There are plenty of things in the real world that are scary. People will experience plenty of suffering during their lives. There are so many unpleasant things we experience on earth, do we really need the fear of eternal torture? I have had people ask me, if I don't believe in hell, how come I don't just steal and murder? The answer to this really stupid question is I don't want to steal and murder. I have definitely met people whom I would rather not exist, but I don't want to kill them. And, sure, there are things I want but cannot afford, but I don't want to steal. I know. I tried. A few times.

When I was thirteen and struggling to make it through hell, I mean middle school, I made a friend whom my mother would describe as a bad influence. While I appreciate my mother's loyalty, and while this girl and I surely did participate in some questionable behavior, I take full responsibility for my own delinquency. To label her as a bad influence would be unfair. However, in honor of my mother, that is how I will refer to her. This friend and I liked to go to the mall. As adolescents, we didn't have much money. Also, as adolescents, we were pre-occupied with boys and sex. So, naturally, we went to the mall with the sole intention of obtaining frilly underwear.

Over the summer between 7th and 8th grade, my bad influence and I would have one of our parents drive us to the mall. As we lived deep into the foothills, this was a bit of a trek. When we finally arrived, we did all the normal things. We stood outside smoking cigarettes looking nowhere near as cool as we thought we were. Even with the hair-sprayed bangs, too-tight jeans, and ridiculously stuffed bras, we still managed to look like the immature children we so desperately wanted to not be. When we were done looking "cool" we would venture inside the sprawling shopping complex.

We would slowly walk through the shops until we found one that sold the undergarments we thought were the sexiest, picking the store that also seemed the busiest. The more people in a store the better. We would then proceed to pick out at least a dozen items, if not more, to take into the dressing room. At that time there was not usually a limit to the number of items you could take into a dressing room. We chose the Grand Suite, otherwise known as the handicapped stall, so that we could go in together.

We tried on the various lacy things and picked out what we wanted. My bad influence was slightly more developed than I, so naturally I went for the amplest padding I could find. We then put on all the things we wanted, at once. Layering the items became a little tricky, as the more you put on the tighter they became. We also had to be aware of how we would look with five pairs of underwear and bras on under our already-suffocating clothing. When we were satisfied, we would then each pick out something cheap to buy and go to the checkout counter after returning the unwanted items to the rack. No one would suspect that as children we would be buying something while simultaneously stealing adult underwear.

This worked perfectly every time. I might even go so far as to say we could be the reason they now have someone checking the number of items as you go into the dressing room, and the number of items you walk out with. You're welcome. As brazen as this was, we were never caught. We even went so far as to steal regular items of clothing like shirts and jeans. I knew it was wrong, and I even felt bad about it deep down. It wasn't until my mom saw all the items I had acquired "on sale" that I finally realized that I couldn't do it anymore.

The last time I stole, my mom had taken me and this not-so-bad influence to the mall to get school clothes. I had the money my dad had sent, which was not much, considering all the things I had come home with. My mom was so proud. She had tried to teach me to be frugal. A good portion of my clothes usually came from either K-Mart or the thrift store. She taught me how to find discounts and clearances, and also to root out the designer clothing buried deep in the racks at the Salvation Army. So, when I came home from the mall with roughly $500 worth of clothes, when I went there with only $100, the look of sheer joy on her face was devastating. That voice in my head that kept telling me I was an asshole for stealing finally broke through. It had been there all along, I just kept telling it to shut the fuck up, as it was not being cool. I could no longer avoid it. It wasn't hell that stopped my criminal spree, it was the look of pride on my mom's face. Not hell, but my own organic sense of conscience.

I felt like an asshole because I was being an asshole. It is that simple. I hated that feeling. As bitter and angry and confused as I was at that age, I knew after only a few short months that I didn't want to be a thief. It wasn't the thought of punishment, eternal or otherwise, that stopped me. It was how rotten it made me feel. Some twenty years later I told my mom what I did, and even after that amount of time, I still felt awful about it.

I would be stretching the truth a bit to say that was the absolute last time I've done something shitty. I have done some other stuff that sucks, but each time, I was reminded by my conscience that I don't like the feeling that comes with doing something shitty. Ultimately, I would rather do things that make me feel good. The simple fact that someone needs to fear retribution to be a good person may just be a really good indicator that that person is an asshole. If the only reason you aren't raping, murdering, or stealing is because you are afraid of punishment, whether on earth or beyond, you could just be an asshole.

Fear and Altruism

Fear has helped humans as a species survive. When we see a snake or other foul disgusting creature that scares us, our first reaction is to recoil, or otherwise remove ourselves from the potential danger. We are programmed to react before determining for certain whether the perceived danger is actually dangerous. That is how we have made it this far. If cavemen had taken the time to see if the huge kitty with really big teeth wanted to cuddle instead of eating us, we would likely not have advanced.

Have you ever walked into a dark room and felt an adrenaline surge because you spotted something nefarious out of the corner of your eye? Only to discover seconds later that it was just a sweatshirt on a rocking chair or some other totally harmless thing? That's your brain trying to ensure you aren't ripped to pieces by a saber tooth tiger. According to Science Daily your amygdala, which are a pair of almond shaped neurons located deep in the temporal lobe of your brain. The amygdala is responsible for processing emotions and our survival instincts. It tends to be overly cautious and will trigger a fight or flight response to what usually turns out to be something benign. Basically, it's your brain saying, "Better to be overly cautious than dead."

Because our sense of fear is what has helped us survive, it can also be easily exploited as a means of control. Enter the concept of hell. We are all inherently afraid of death, so what, then, is worse than death? Infinite pain. No one knows for sure what happens when we die, so why not invent a place so awful that we would do everything to avoid it? If you can convince a person there is a place so bad that it is even worse than death, you can get them to do all sorts of things. A perfect mechanism for controlling behavior. Then you convince them that even questioning its very existence can lead you to be sent there. Absolutely diabolical. Ask questions? Go to hell. Refuse to obey? Go to hell.

The avoidance of hell can be a fantastic justification for all sorts of fucked up things. In fact, if you know that someone you love is going to go to hell, isn't it your absolute duty to save them from it? Take the case of John List. In the early 70s, John decided that his family was starting to turn away from God. He was convinced they would be sent to hell. So, as an ultimate gesture of kindness, he systematically shot each one of his children and his wife and placed them in a large room in his house. He also killed his mother, but was unable to move her body, so he left her upstairs. Then he put on some classical music, turned the thermostat as low as it could go, and left to live out the rest of his virtuous life elsewhere.

He changed his name, remarried, and lived a remarkably uneventful life. When he was caught, decades later, everyone including his new wife was shocked to learn of his crimes. Shocked, I tell you. He went to church regularly and everything. He believed he did nothing wrong. In fact, he saved all of his family's souls from burning in a lake of fire for all of eternity. Did he really, though? Maybe, just possibly, he was tired of his teenagers, wife, and mother, and found a terrific excuse for getting out of the life he didn't want anymore, using the very convenient concept of hell. He did save a lot in child support and alimony, I suppose.

There is also the case of Andrea Yates, who drowned all five of her children in order to save them from hell. I won't go into the details of that one because whether mentally ill or not I can barely stand to think of it, and it makes me as mad as, well, hell. The idea of hell is abhorrent and very obviously a failure in its attempt to regulate human behavior. It seems like it may be a motivator for very bad behavior in the case of someone who is mentally ill, or otherwise lacking a sense of empathy.

Humans generally have a strong sense of altruism and empathy that has also helped us to survive as a species. Altruism is basically when you do something nice for someone without the expectation of getting anything in return. Empathy is being able to put yourself in someone else's shoes, trying to understand how they might feel. These two tendencies work to our advantage in many ways. They stop most people from doing shitty things and help us to be successful in the world. People like John and Andrea are, for the most part, thankfully the exception.

If every time someone cut you off on the freeway you followed them home and killed them, humans would not be nearly as successful. Yes, we do fucked up things to each other, but generally speaking, we do much better when we take care of each other. It is simply better for our own survival if we don't murder someone who is holding up the line at the checkout in the grocery store. Being nice to each other benefits everyone.

While altruism in humans played a huge part in the evolution and success of our species as a whole, it can be hard to see on an everyday basis. What gets reported widely in the media is largely negative and would lead one to suspect that almost all people suck. That is very much not reality, thankfully. Unfortunately, violence and negativity simply get more clicks and ratings than do random acts of altruism. The NBC Nightly News almost always ends its show with a positive, nice piece that is supposed to make the rest of the news seem not so bad. It is, in my opinion, rarely successful. People being assholes simply makes more interesting news, hence the saying, "If it bleeds, it leads."

The truth is, we are actually living in the most peaceful time in our existence. Yes, you read that correctly, I promise, I even double checked. Most people are inherently empathetic and altruistic. They just are, even if they are only driven by a primitive need to survive as a species. Humans as a whole are really pretty nice. It just happens that the assholes around us stand out more. They just make better news.

If you shift your focus just a little and try to notice the nice things people do for each other, you might be surprised. You might just start to see how much kindness actually exists in the world – the guy who lets you go ahead in the checkout line, or maybe the person who waves you in when you are trying to merge in traffic. The little things we do for each other every day that seem inconsequential are really very significant. I swear it happens more often than you think.

Even in the strip club we manage to be nice to each other. I have personally experienced an overwhelming sense of empathy and altruism. Maybe the most notable was back when I was dancing to make enough money to attend culinary school. Because I went to school five days a week, I could only work the club on Saturday night. In just that one night I needed to make all the money I would need for food, gas, and expenses for the whole week. One night I utterly failed to do that and broke into tears close to closing time. A few minutes after, someone asked me what was wrong. They came back with a collection of cash from a bunch of girls. Strippers all donated a little money so that I could go to school that week and stop my blubbering. That really happened. Stripper altruism.

There are many other stories I can tell about kindness in the strip club, like after the declaration of war in Iraq after 9/11. Most of the girls helped put a huge care package together for the troops overseas. It was mostly pornography, panties, and a few snacks, but the thought was there. The world we live in can seem pretty harsh most of the time, but if you stop for a moment and look around, you might just start to see altruism in some unlikely places. We really don't need the concept of hell at all. Deep down people really want to do good things, we have literally evolved that way. It simply feels good to do good, and it feels bad to do bad. The next time you do something selfless for someone, notice how it feels, probably pretty good. Pay attention and you will see how many other of your fellow primates also take the time to do something nice, just because they can.

Chapter 12

Confirming Your Bias

How to Develop a Strong Self-Awareness

Growing up in the eighties, parents urgently warned children that strangers could be dangerous. So, naturally, I was wary of people I had not met before, which mostly meant I was a very difficult charge. To be honest, I'm still a difficult charge. This skepticism led me to make some rash assumptions about people from the instant I met them, assumptions which were often wrong. Learning to identify when I was wrongly perceiving people didn't happen overnight, but over several years, and took a few potent lessons. One of the most memorable happened when my mom left me at a new babysitter's house for the first time.

I was six years old, in this stranger's house. All I wanted to do was go home. There were other children there, but I didn't know them. They weren't at all as upset as I was, for some reason. I was really afraid. I had a hard time understanding why they weren't. Where the other kids saw a kindly looking Latina grandma, I saw a horrid, old witch. No, a real witch. A scary, dangerous witch. I was convinced. The odd mole on her right cheek with a single hair jutting from it was proof enough for me.

At first glance, the house seemed warm and inviting, but underneath it had an odor of warm milk and onions. Sesame Street was playing on a small black and white TV in the corner. Normally Count von Count counting his bats wouldn't have seemed scary, but in my distress, I found him to be profoundly disturbing.

In the backyard, there was a small wooden shed, which my mind told me was also scary. It looked to me like a perfect place to perform witch rituals. I looked in and was just able to make out several large hooks on the wall inside, along with a shovel. My mind immediately went to the most sinister things I could think of. I had quite the imagination as a kid, so naturally I started to panic. Everything I saw from that point on took on a dark quality that fueled my melodramatic misinterpretations.

Right around 11am she called us to lunch. I gathered around the table with the other kids. I had decided at that point that whatever lunch was going to be, I wasn't going to eat it. As my lunch was placed in front of me, I was relieved to see that it was Kraft macaroni and cheese. My relief was soon replaced by horror when I saw something odd hidden in the noodles. I lifted my fork to smell it and was devastated to find that it was....... tuna, the single grossest thing on the planet. I just sat there and sulked, even though I was starving.

I was starting to feel sleepy. I drank my juice, but then I imagined a connection between the juice and my sleepiness. So, poison, obviously. Then I noticed the other kids were starting to look sleepy, as well. All eyes growing heavy, she directed everyone to the living room where we found blankets on the floor. The other kids started to lay down. I was in no mood to comply.

It was then that I started to yell. And yell, and yell. I came up with all manner of insults. "You're stinky, old and ugly," and every other foul thing I could think of. I was upsetting the other kids, so I quickly found myself alone in a strange bedroom.

"You'll feel better after a nap," my babysitter cackled.

About an hour later I awoke to a soft creak as the door opened. The sweet little lady asked me how I was feeling. The witch's robe I had imagined now appeared as it really was, a sundress, covered in cheery looking daisies. Her voice, soft and reassuring. She came over to me, put a hand on my shoulder, then folded me in her arms and gave me a hug. I was instantly immersed in a warm cloud of love. I had fallen asleep panicked that I would be carved up for parts. But when I awoke, things looked very different. I checked – I had no stitches. I was hungry, but otherwise OK. She then asked if I wanted a snack.

Mrs. C fixed me a peanut butter and jelly sandwich with some apple slices. When I finished, she smiled, told me to go play, and that my mom would be there in a couple hours. I went out to the yard. The shed I had thought was used to torture little children now looked like the garden shed it really was. The house still smelled vaguely of onions, but no longer seemed as menacing as when I first arrived. I realized how mistaken I had been. I had misread all the signs to fit my imagination. Despite her unfortunate mole, she was only a little, old Mexican grandma, running a small daycare out of her home. In my six-year-old anger and confusion, I had actually perceived this nice lady to be an actual, dangerous witch. All I really needed was a sandwich and a nap to see it all over again with new eyes.

Self-Deception

While this might seem like an extreme case of a child's wayward imagination, wrongly perceiving a situation is not limited to children. Quite the opposite, in fact. Adults are even worse. Why, you ask? Because when an adult misjudges a situation, they are much more certain that they are right. *I'm a grown up, obviously I'm not mistaken.* It's likely I am mistaken just the same, but it's much harder to realize and then admit you're wrong when you're an adult.

It might seem like our brains are just one big mess of anxieties, biases, and misunderstandings because that's exactly what they are. Our perception of the reality we exist in gets filtered through our very imperfect brains. Part of that is a defense mechanism that helps keep us safe, and part of it is a product of our collective life experience and our genetic makeup. We are pretty much doomed to perceive reality in a way that is not correct. That does not necessarily mean we won't ever be able to parse the truth from our slanted view of the world. It just means we need to be a little more diligent in how we evaluate the information we take in.

This is especially true when it comes to social interactions. I am definitely guilty of judging people and situations in the wrong way. As a dancer, I relied on my perceptions to guide how I acted and to whom I spoke. If I'm having a bad night, I may look at other dancers negatively who seem to be doing well. I may think they are doing something dirty in the VIP room, without actually seeing them do anything wrong. In reality, they might just be better at convincing someone to get a lap dance. My mind is trying to protect my ego. If I start to think the problem is me and not a clandestine hooker invading my club, it will feed my insecurity. I am essentially taking the focus off myself so that I don't slide into a swamp of self-pity. My ego can be so defensive that even if I am consciously aware of my own bias, I still struggle to stop myself from trying to place the blame somewhere else.

Our brains try to process quickly to make sure we react swiftly to danger, as opposed to taking time to digest the information. This mechanism practically guarantees that we misinterpret most situations right out of the gate. Someone's tone of voice or gestures can seem malicious until we get a little more information, only to realize we have fooled ourselves into thinking this person sucks. A majority of my good friends are people I thought were assholes when I first met them. I tend to think people will judge me for my profession or what I look like, so I am very skeptical when I first meet people. My default position is to assume everyone I meet is judging me harshly. Spoiler alert, they aren't. I'm the judgmental one. The bias my brain has created leads me to a false perception. For me to function in society and not be a total bitch, I have to constantly remind myself that my perception could be wrong. It isn't always, but most of the time it is. It's kind of a bummer to have to admit that I am, in fact, the asshole, not the other person. Being able to acknowledge my own bias is what makes me able to override it, which has ultimately led to many good friendships.

There was a bouncer I worked with years ago. He was an asshole. He was sarcastic, snarky, and an insufferable smart-ass. I dreaded having to talk to him, but even more, I hated that I had to tip him. For almost two years I avoided him, talked shit about him when I could, and was an asshole back to him. Other girls didn't seem to have a problem with this guy, though I simply couldn't figure out why not. One day I finally confronted him and said, "Why are you such an asshole?"

I was caught completely off guard when he turned the question back to me, "Why are *you* such an asshole?" I had to take a moment to clutch my hypothetical pearls before considering the question. My mind took a minute to recall our previous interactions.

100

It had never occurred to me that maybe I had been the asshole in this whole relationship. All of my own sarcastic, snarky, and smart-ass comments suddenly came flooding back to me. It became clear he had simply been feeding me back my own bullshit. I had thoroughly misperceived this guy as an asshole. It was then that I discovered I really liked this guy.

He turned out to be exactly the kind of asshole I was, and in our mutual asshole-ish-ness, we became friends. As a strip club bouncer, he had developed his own bias. He was just as afraid of being judged harshly as I was and as a result of our respective biases, we mirrored each other's attitudes. I spent two years projecting unnecessary animosity toward someone with whom I actually had much more in common than I wanted to recognize. After this epiphany, we spent our shifts together being assholes to everyone else. We created an asshole alliance, totally failing to apply the lesson we learned together to other people.

Unfortunately, he was involved in a freak electrical accident about six months after we became friends and passed away. His funeral was an especially hard one. I felt stupid for missing out on a friendship because I was so caught up in my misperception of him for two years. I had thought we would have more time. After he was gone, I realized how much my bias distorts my perception of people when I first meet them. I decided I would do my best to not let my own issues color the way I viewed people. I would be a liar if I said I am always successful, but I do try to remember not to judge someone right away.

Cognitive Bias and Logical Fallacies

There are all kinds of cognitive biases that shape our perception of the world. Some are actually helpful. The bias I describe in misinterpreting social interactions is mostly confirmation bias. This makes us see information that confirms what we already believe and ignore information that might counter it – like thinking my bouncer was a judgmental asshole, or that my babysitter was a witch. What I already believed and what I wanted to believe made me ignore information that didn't fit those beliefs.

I actually saw things that were not real, such as the hooks in the garden shed being meant for hanging children and not garden tools.

Problems arise when we make decisions based on biases even when we actually have the time to consider the evidence. For instance, let's say you are looking to buy a washing machine and your friend has told you that their new low water model is the best they have ever owned. Their opinion of their purchase might create a confirmation bias in your own mind that a low water washing machine is the best one. You may not actually take the time now to research them, as you might have otherwise. You could learn later that these washers might have a tendency to break down and require regular maintenance to stop them from smelling like a bucket of buttholes. This would be considered to be an anchoring bias, where we take the first piece of information we get and stop looking for more.

When I look to place blame on another dancer for my own slow night, this is a self-serving bias. Instead of focusing on myself, it is easier to look to external forces to explain my bad fortune. On the flip side, if I am having a good night, I give myself all the credit. "Bad" equals something or someone else's fault. "Good" equals I am awesome. Before learning about cognitive biases, I chalked this kind of thinking up to my own desire to preserve my vanity. While that is true, it could also be the case that hookers really do interfere with my profits, although I have exactly zero objective evidence of it. And that, my friends, is exactly how easy it is to continue well established self-serving bias.

A healthy sense of skepticism toward our own perceptions is the best way to overcome irrational biases. Taking a step back, even if only for a moment, can help you identify where you may be letting preconceived ideas influence your perception of a situation. Understanding that your brain has a tendency to give more weight to only certain information can help you reevaluate that information. It takes some practice and a lot of self-awareness. Practicing skepticism toward your own conclusions is not always easy, but if done consistently, it can become a habit.

Cognitive biases can lead to logical fallacies. When I saw the mole on my babysitter's face, I thought it was proof she was a witch. Most of the witches I had encountered through stories and TV had moles on their faces, therefore she was a witch. At age six, I was suspicious of any person I did not know and that led me to look for any evidence to confirm that bias. Face moles are not evidence of witchcraft, but I deceived myself with this logical fallacy to confirm my bias. We are almost set up to deceive ourselves with flawed logic. Once you recognize your own flawed logic, you can start to avoid these kinds of self-deception.

Logical fallacies are most often used to bolster one side of an argument. Saying someone is Hitler because they have a tiny mustache is a logical fallacy. Mustaches don't equal Hitler, although, when I see a large mustache, I have to stop myself from thinking "porn star". That is my own logical fallacy based on the number of mustached porn stars I have seen. Even if you are able to recognize a logical fallacy in an argument, it may not be as apparent when it is in your own thoughts.

These common flaws in our everyday thought processes are what can make us perceive situations and people in a way that is not reality. Physical factors such as hormone fluctuations (not just for women by the way), stress, pain, and even hunger can alter the way we view the world. Because I work out a lot, I tend to have consistent aches and pains, and can also get ravenously hungry. If you are the customer service representative of a company with whom I have a minor beef, you do not want to talk to me when my knee hurts and I am starving. In that particular state, I'm a monster, and any minor mistake you or your company may have made becomes cataclysmic in my eyes. In reality, it may have simply been an innocent oversight, but I will perceive it as a big fucking deal. Later, after some ibuprofen and a sandwich, I may come to understand that I may have overreacted just a tad. My compromised physical state makes me unable to see that I am giving in to the cognitive bias I have that all customer service reps are morons, and a simple mistake means a grand conspiracy to piss me off. My bad. For what it is worth, I now make an effort not to deal with personal business on an empty stomach.

Emotions, along with physical factors, all contribute to an unrealistic view of reality. Developing a strong sense of self-awareness is the best way to get past our cognitive biases and have a clearer view of the things around us. Sometimes just being able to admit when we are wrong about a person or a situation that we have perceived inaccurately can help us be more grounded in our own world view and how we view other people. What matters is that we learn to accept that we are more prone to being wrong than we would like to admit. Then we are able to change our minds based on objective facts instead of what our flawed brains want us to believe.

Do you perhaps have a bias that may help you see the world inaccurately? Maybe stemming from what you were taught, or a circumstance that makes you feel one way or another regardless of the information you are taking in? Are you instantly annoyed when you walk into a DMV because one time you had to wait a long time? Does the guy with a tiny little mustache and a German accent seem like a psychopath hell bent on genocide? Is that stripper you just met really an idiot hooker on drugs? Take a moment to consider if you are evaluating evidence objectively or through an irrational cognitive bias. Sometimes discovering that you are wrong can be wonderfully enlightening.

Chapter 13

Get Lucky

Uncover Your Secret Superstitions

Last night at the club was awesome, and I'm feeling like one lucky stripper this morning. The sun is shining, the birds are chirping, my hair is fabulous. So fabulous in fact, it will only take about half the amount of time to get ready for work later. As I stroll, I come upon a little kitty who stops for just a moment at the kissy sound I make, long enough to allow me to pet him. He crosses in front of me and I continue my walk, smiling just a little at the cute little bugger. Up ahead, I spy a painter on a ladder. I walk under it with a quick step and casual greeting to the workman at the top.

It is then I start to notice a few dark clouds overhead. Before I left, I contemplated taking my umbrella but looked at the sunshine and left it at home. I had opened it in the kitchen just to make sure it was functioning, and as I did, I knocked the salt shaker off the counter. Spilling salt is bad luck, no biggie, though, as I threw a little pinch over my shoulder to counteract it. While I was tossing the salt over my shoulder, I just happened to brush against a mirror on the wall and sent it crashing to the floor. Doesn't that mean seven years of bad luck? The clouds grow more ominous as I recount this morning's events. Was the cat I just petted all black? It was. At that thought, a sour taste suddenly becomes noticeable in my mouth to complement the knot that just appeared in my stomach.

Sure enough, the sky opens up and in an instant I'm soaked. I run back under the ladder just in time to hear the painter curse as his work is ruined by the rain, along with my fabulous strip club-ready hair. A pebble jumps under my shoe and sends me sprawling to the ground. I pick myself up to discover that my favorite jeans have ripped, and not in a fashionable place either, but right in the crotch. A small silver lining may be that I didn't scrape myself. A Band-Aid on a stripper is a not a good look. Finally, I make it to my front door only to discover that my house key must have escaped from my pocket when I fell. I lift up the fake rock that should hold a spare only to remember I gave it to my friend to feed my cats the last time I left for the weekend. Shit. It's starting to hail so I walk around to the back slider which is standing wide open. I remember stepping outside this morning to check the weather and must have forgotten to close it. I see the wind and rain have strewn wet leaves and debris all over my new rug. Thinking it couldn't get any worse, I wonder, "Where did all this go south?" I even remembered to wish on the shooting star I saw the night before.

Was it opening the umbrella inside, spilling the salt, breaking the mirror? That fucking black cat perhaps? Maybe walking under the ladder, or could it be Friday the 13th? That must be it, the unluckiest of all days. I have been cursed. All these things lined up and now I am suffering the consequences. The universe is working against me. What do I do now? First, clean up, then get back in bed and wait it out. But the mirror, will this last the whole seven years? I knock on wood in a futile attempt to counteract all the bad luck that is sure to come. Then I remember a tails up penny I found, like the cherry on a turd sundae of bad luck. I'm now sure I am doomed. Fuck all this bad luck and fuck my life.

Superstitions

If the above sounds stupid and ridiculous, congratulations, you're not a dumbass. Humans have believed all sorts of stupid things for a very long time. In our attempts to make sense of a world that can seem chaotic and dangerous, we make up some crazy shit to explain it all. When we lack a sense of control, superstitions can help us feel just a bit better, however irrational. Lack of control leads to anxiety, which is only heightened when we can't explain the things that make us anxious.

People who claim to not be superstitious might still take a moment to consider if they should step outside before they open an umbrella, even though it may make more sense to open it inside to ensure they don't catch any sprinkles as they exit the door. Throwing salt on the floor somehow could seem appropriate after spilling some, even though you are essentially just making a bigger mess. If someone were to spill something on my floor, and then proceed to throw more of that something on the floor, I would ask them to leave.

The idea that black cats are somehow dangerous led to many black cats being systematically killed during the Dark Ages and beyond. My family adopted a black cat a few years ago, who crosses our paths on a daily basis. We haven't seemed to have had any more bad luck than usual. Ironically, the cat is the one who seems plagued by fear of the mundane. She came from a shelter and we suspect that she was feral at one point, which would explain her abject terror at everyday occurrences. Without knowing her early life experiences, her behavior could be easily explained by a feeling of insecurity out in the world. We affectionately call her our dumpster kitty. She probably has good reason to be suspicious and overly cautious. As humans, it is utterly irrational to consider her detrimental to our potential good fortunes. On Halloween night, we take precautions to make sure she stays inside, because there are humans who would really like to kill her because of her seemingly bad luck. In this case, it would seem that the black cat is the more rational being.

Many superstitions are benign, although I think it would be safe to assume that black cats would disagree with that statement. Not washing your lucky socks for fear of removing their luckiness probably won't hurt you. It may interfere with your love life, however. For the most part, our silly magical beliefs in small, little rituals don't affect us one way or the other, except maybe to give us a little more confidence that things may go our way. There is actual evidence that when people engage in their superstitions it affects their mind set and could help them perform better, if only because they think it's helping. I think it would be fair to assume that your smelly socks didn't play a part in your softball victory, but that slight boost of confidence may have.

Superstitions are an example of magical thinking. One form of magical thinking is believing that one's hopes and desires can somehow affect the outcome of certain events. If you find a penny that is heads up and then win $2 on a scratcher, you might be tempted to correlate the two events. Our tendency to correlate unrelated events dates back to our caveman days. That, much like the rest of our irrational thinking, is simply the drive to understand a world that we may never fully comprehend, and also goes back to our development and survival as primitive humans. The lack of control we inevitably feel about things we can't explain makes us believe some pretty ridiculous things.

Magical thinking, as it relates to the psychological disorder OCD or obsessive-compulsive disorder, is an example of magical thinking gone astray. This disorder can develop when magical thinking gets way out of hand, usually driven by anxiety. The fear that without performing certain rituals something bad will happen can become debilitating. The rituals may not involve the common superstitious rituals we are most familiar with but are the same type of magical thinking. Maybe someone has become obsessed with the idea that the house will burn down if they don't flick the light switch a certain number of times. That irrational idea is in the same vein as believing some misfortune will happen if you open an umbrella inside. Magical thinking gives people the illusion of control. Rituals provide the comfort of thinking you have somehow disarmed the potential bad luck, reinforcing that illusion.

Our brains have evolved to pick up on patterns, even where none exist. Recognizing patterns is another example of how our species made it this far in the first place. At some point, a person noticed that if they ate a certain type of plant, they got sick. After a few times this pattern revealed itself. Making such connections is for the most part helpful. When in the strip club, I would definitely look for patterns, and then make correlations whether correct or not, to determine whether to approach someone for a lap dance. Over the years, I was finally able to understand that most of the correlations or patterns I made were largely inaccurate. Sexual attraction seems to be a difficult thing to predict, but that didn't seem to stop my silly brain from wanting to act on false correlations.

Early on in my illustrious career as a nude dancer, a girl I admired told me to look at a guy's shoes. She was adamant that a man's shoes would always reveal their net worth and how likely they were to want a VIP dance. From that moment on, shoes became the way I would prioritize the men I would approach. A nice pair of loafers meant money. Sneakers on the other hand, meant forget about it, he is not worth my time. I got to the point where I would only approach loafers, and therefore only danced for guys in loafers. Loafers meant VIP money. The flaw in my logic went undiscovered because I simply didn't bother with those low-lifes in Nikes.

Until one fateful night, there were...gasp...no loafers to be found. I was going to starve. I had no choice but to approach a downtrodden man in worn Adidas. He was terribly ordinary and obviously low middle class, but what the hell, I had bills to pay. I walked up to him and gave my regular spiel, and to my utter amazement he said, "Yes." We went to the VIP for what I was sure to be only one dance, but I was surprised yet again. This man in sneakers ended up being one of the most lucrative men I would dance for, and not just that night, but my whole career. I had fallen victim to stripper magical thinking.

Not only have we evolved to look for patterns, but our minds are highly suggestible. So, when someone I thought I could trust told me that a guy's shoes were the best indicator of someone with money, I bought it, hook, line, and sinker. Even if I had doubted her, it's highly likely I would have made the connection in my own experiences, anyway. That little bit of information made me notice a pattern that most of the guys I danced for had those kinds of shoes, not realizing I was pretty much only asking those guys. I was basically reinforcing my belief by avoiding guys with shoes that seemed cheap and didn't fit the pattern I mistakenly associated with obtaining VIP dances. I made my own sort of superstition that I was afraid to stray from, likely losing a lot of money.

Once I started to ask all the guys, loafers, sneakers, and brace yourself... flip flops, what I noticed was that shoes had absolutely no bearing on the likelihood of a guy accepting my proposal for a VIP dance or how many dances he ended up getting. Another thing I noticed, was that the girl who told me about the shoes in the first place asked everyone also. Regardless of footwear. That was when I had another stripper epiphany. I believed she may have told me about the shoes to increase her own customer pool. By discouraging me from asking certain customers she decreased her own competition. She had a whole category of customer that she knew I wouldn't ask, thereby eliminating me as a competitor for those customers. Remember when I told you that not all strippers were dumb?

Even after that lesson, that correlation does not equal causation, I still had a propensity to find patterns and correlations where none existed. I started to notice that bald men seemed to be particularly fond of me, so I started to ask them first. Basically, repeating the irrational shoe fallacy all over again. Once I realized that I was doing it again, I stopped, and so did the pattern of bald guys tending to like me more than men with a full head of hair, proving to myself yet again that my brain was bound and determined to lead me to false conclusions.

Creating a superstitious belief is incredibly easy because we are simply predisposed to do it. We are just built that way. Even the smartest and most educated among us are not immune. Once an idea gets planted in our heads – like breaking a mirror or spilling salt causes bad things to happen – it can be really hard to overcome, even if you are consciously aware of how goofy the idea is. Welcome to your ridiculous brain.

Letting Go of Magical Thinking

Why is it so hard to let go of our superstitions? Because they offer some comfort and reassurance in an otherwise mostly unpredictable world. Believing we have some control where we actually don't can ease our anxiety about all sorts of situations. For instance, if you experience fear that you will have bad luck because you knocked the salt shaker over, you can simply throw a pinch over your shoulder to negate the bad luck. It is an instant remedy to your anxiety. An irrational solution to an irrational problem.

As kids, we are prone to magical thinking. Santa Claus, the tooth fairy, and the Easter bunny are only a few examples of childhood magical thinking. When the truth is finally accepted that those things are not real, it seems that our adult minds simply find more "grown up" magical things to believe in. Just because you might think a superstition such as walking under a ladder may seem more mature, doesn't mean it is any less bullshit than the tooth fairy.

We take solace in the thought that some force or magic is on our side. Our supernatural cheerleader, if you will. It just feels good to think the universe is somehow pulling for us. Your

110

disgusting lucky socks have somehow been imparted with a magical power to help your team win. Not really. They're just the filthy socks you happened to be wearing when your team won. That's it. It's not luck, karma, or the universe wanting you to win. Your filthy socks are simply filthy socks.

But why should we give up these beliefs if they make us feel good? Because at some point this kind of magical thinking can and will most likely backfire on you. Like me thinking that only guys in loafers will want VIP dances, I lost out on many lucrative opportunities. While I didn't really think there was something magical about loafers, I did give them an unwarranted amount of power over my money. Just as giving mirrors or umbrellas more power to influence a situation than they deserve, which like loafers, is absolutely none.

What happens to your thoughts if, for instance, your superstition proves wrong? What if you find a penny heads up and then get in a car accident? Is the universe out to get you? If you spill salt and throw a pinch over your shoulder, then get a cancer diagnosis? What then? You followed the rules of the superstition and it failed. Do you then see the events that happen to you as hopeless? You are rendered completely powerless. If your bad luck means your favorite sports team didn't make the playoffs, no big deal, but what if your magical thinking applied to more consequential life events?

If you really believed that stepping on a crack would break your mom's back, and your mom actually broke her back, would you blame yourself? That is kind of goofy, but people put their faith in things just as goofy. Many pseudo sciences rely on just that kind of faith. Iridology, for example, is the belief that illness can be diagnosed by examining someone's iris. If your belief is that strong, you may forego actual medical treatment. And if your iridologist is unsuccessful in treating your illness, you may just think that was what the universe wanted for you.

Magical thinking can be a slippery slope. One moment it's just lucky dirty socks, the next it could be some conman guru convincing you that your luck will improve if you only cleanse your aura. He can help you do it for a nominal fee compared to how much he can get you to give. Magical thinking can leave you vulnerable to all sorts of scams and fallacies. Like wholeheartedly believing that your mentor stripper has your best interests in mind, while she's making a killing dancing for guys in Converse.

A world without magic and superstition may sound like a barren land of logic and reason. No Santa Claus, the Easter bunny, or the tooth fairy to bring wonder to an otherwise logical universe. If there is no karma making your high school sweetheart miserable after they cheated on you, where is the justice in the world? How lonely and dull is your life without magic? It is exactly as lonely and dull as you want it to be.

While it's true there are a ton of things you can't control, there are just as many that you can. Looking at the stars can be just as wonderful and awe-inspiring even when you know they don't have an ounce of influence on your life. Finding the truth about our world and everything in it can be just as comforting as making shit up. When I discovered that a guy's shoes had no bearing on whether he would want a dance or not, a whole new world of sneakers and flip flops opened up to me. I was no longer a slave to loafers. I might ask you to take just a tiny challenge. Think of a superstition you actively engage in and see what happens if you don't perform the ritual. Refrain for a significant amount of time to confirm your conclusions, maybe even take a moment to jot down the results. I would be willing to bet that you discover your ritualistic thinking has no bearing whatsoever on your luck.

Sometimes you may have superstitions or behaviors you might not even be consciously aware of. We get used to doing things with the worry in the back of our minds that if we don't do them, things may not go the way we want them to. I know that opening an umbrella indoors won't cause any harm or future bad luck, and yet I am reluctant to do so. The rational part of my brain explains this as, maybe I'll knock something over if I do. I think somewhere deep down in my mind I'm afraid something more catastrophic could happen if were to brazenly disregard this superstition. Is there a superstition you have hiding in the recesses of your head that stops you from doing certain things? I challenge you to explore this idea. You may be surprised to find out that you are unknowingly acting on a superstition you didn't think you had.

To learn that you are in control of your own life and destiny is one of the most empowering things you can do for yourself. Knowing you are free to adopt a black cat, walk under ladders, and decorate your house with broken mirrors and open umbrellas is as liberating as taking your bra off after a long day. Not only are you free from the consequences of bad luck, you are free from the rituals that provide good luck. You won't have your supernatural cheerleader, but you also won't have to live with the idea that your cheerleader has turned on you and is now rooting for you to fail. You are neither blessed nor cursed. If you want to win your softball game you don't have to put on a moldy pair of socks, you just need to practice.

Living your life according to logic and reason may sound boring and cynical, but it really isn't. The world is plenty interesting, wonderful, and amazing without goofy magical superstitions. Not every event whether positive or negative has some clandestine cause or meaning, sometimes shit just happens. So, do us all a favor and trash those smelly socks.

Chapter 14

Are You Psychic?

Question Everything

Perched on my six-inch heels, I survey the crowd. From my vantage point, I can see the entire room. The mirror on the far side allows me to also keep an eye on the front entrance located behind me. In my head I have a list of prioritizing criteria that I use to choose my next mark. Ideally, he will be in his mid-40s, dressed in business casual attire, and will have a slightly bewildered look on his face. During the week, the clientele generally comes from out of town. He is here on business, away from his family, and bored to death in his hotel room. He doesn't know the city, or the club.

I spot my mark in the mirror. Middle aged, moderately dressed and with the appropriate expression of wonder. He's at the front counter forking over the cover charge before obediently offering his arm to allow the sickeningly sweet door girl to fit him with his wristband. He immediately heads toward the bathroom. I wait patiently for him to return and find a seat. The way he scans the room to choose a seat confirms what I already suspect, that this is his first time here. He chooses a seat close enough to the stage to observe, but far enough away that he won't be expected to tip. I can safely assume he is well versed in the strip club scene.

Timing right now is crucial. I need to give him enough time to get a drink and get just a little settled. A very young dancer approaches him immediately. Perfect, I can see right away that he is annoyed by her aggressive approach and over-eagerness. She walks away looking dejected and wobbly on her heels. The waitress brings him a bottled water and I see that he tips her generously. Almost salivating, I have to repress my urge to approach. With the patience of a hungry cougar, I watch him watch the stage with little interest. He sips his water and scans the room, his eyes land on me for a moment. I pretend to be looking elsewhere as I keep him in my field of vision. His eyes are fixed on me just long enough for me to be fairly confident that he likes what he sees.

I wait another moment before I start to slowly and confidently saunter in his direction, appearing to just notice him. I smile as I approach, and he smiles back. I kneel down to be eye level and say, "Hello." The game begins.

He replies, "Hello, how are you tonight?"

I say, "Fabulous, and you?"

He says he's fine. We exchange our names and a brief handshake. His hands are smooth. He's wearing a gold wedding band. I start to tell him what I already know about him. He's from out of town on business, bored in his hotel room. Each response gives me another clue. I subtly repeat back the things I know about him, and ask him if he's ready to play, knowing the answer. We walk back to the VIP where I continue my schtick. Forty-five minutes and hundreds of dollars later we emerge from the back room and return to the main floor. I give him a hug and tell him to come back on his next trip. He tells me how amazed he is that I can know him so well and says, "It's like you're psychic."

"That's because I am," I say with a wink and smile. "See you next time."

As I retreat to the dressing room with my spoils, I take a moment to reflect on my conquest. I was able to tell him where he was from, what he did, a good portion of his upbringing, level of education, I was even able to tell him what branch of the military he served in. The look of amazement grew with every new revelation. He simply couldn't believe how I could know these things. By the time our encounter ended, he really thought I may have possessed supernatural powers. Spoiler alert, I'm about as psychic as a wind sock.

Stone Cold Reading

We all like to feel connected to someone. Especially people in a situation that is unfamiliar, lonely, or even just boring. Enter the strip club customer. My job is to provide entertainment and a cure for boredom. One of the best ways to do that is by creating a sense of a personal connection. My recounting of my techniques or schtick may come across as cold and calculating. While it definitely is, there is a sign on the outside of the entrance stating that what happens inside is for entertainment purposes only. I believe this is the main difference between what I do and traditional psychics and mediums. Although, I will concede, I may be using the fact that customers are warned to know better as a salve for my own conscience. It could be, just maybe, that I am no better than your average fortune teller charlatan.

While some commercial psychics might display this disclaimer, most don't. If you look carefully in the fine print, you might see it, but like all fine print, it is designed to go unnoticed. Psychics and strippers are not often looked at as having much in common, except maybe in unusual wardrobe choices. But the best and most successful strippers use the same tricks and techniques as our famous not-so-Jamaican friend Miss Cleo of the Psychic Readers Network used. Psychics and mediums are not usually required to state that their services are for entertainment. Some choose to, simply to help avoid financial liability in case of a lawsuit. Some psychics and mediums also try to use religious freedom as cover and a way to obtain tax exemption. I'm fairly certain that I've given a few men a seemingly religious experience, but I highly doubt the IRS would allow me a religious tax break.

There are a few common techniques used in readings. Cold reading is probably the most common. Cold reading is basically using information like body language, clothing, education, and other superficial information to imply that the reader knows much more about a person than they should. For example, guys are usually surprised to hear me say this is their first time there. A fact that is outwardly obvious by their body language. The second most astonishing thing I seem to know is that they are there on business, which is another extremely easy thing to surmise simply based on their clothing. Someone who lives in town is less likely to show up in slacks and a tie. Of course, just because someone is in slacks doesn't mean he's from out of town, but it is more probable than not.

Cold readings are based on probability. When attempting to amaze a potential client, I start with vague but highly likely assumptions. Then, based on the response, either verbal or physical, I narrow down the "predictions" until I get a hit. If I make an assumption that is incorrect, I simply move on quickly, using the error to better direct the conversation. In most cases, the mark will forget the wrong predictions and remember the right ones. If you have ever watched a so-called psychic reading, you will notice that the reader may start by asking questions about a relative or acquaintance whose name starts with an M or a J, two of the most common letters to begin a name. They give the choice between relative or acquaintance to broaden the association. When you say "yes" they then move on to say, "You were close to this person." Each response or confirmation leads to a narrowing down of the predictions. If you walked into the whole thing expecting or hoping that they had some kind of magical power, their predictions then may seem not only accurate, but supernatural. I promise they're not.

Newspaper horoscopes, fortune cookies, or even Nostradamus' seemingly accurate predictions all rely on our tendency to make associations where none actually exist. Psychics use the same tactics, but they can seem more miraculous because they're done in person, and therefore seem more personal. One good informational hit, and you're set up to believe anything else they are saying.

My favorite Chinese restaurant has paper placemats that give the animals for your year of birth, otherwise known as the Chinese zodiac. Mine, being the horse, says, "Pays attention to appearance and likes to dress up beautifully. Insightful, act quickly, highly independent, as well as popular and attractive to the opposite sex." How can I argue with that obviously spot-on description of me? Well, how about this one? "Quick witted, smart, charming and persuasive" or "Popular, compassionate, and sincere." So, am I a rat, a horse, or a rabbit? If I look at all the animals, I could in fact find character traits in all of them that I could relate to. Crack open the fortune cookie to reveal that I have good luck coming to me shortly, and I might just start to convince myself that there is something to this whole Chinese zodiac thing.

As for psychic strippers and fortune tellers at the county fair, most people don't take this stuff seriously. It's all for fun. What harm could this kind of entertainment possibly do?

Grief for Profit

It turns out, quite a lot of harm, indeed. While I may take advantage of an out of town businessman's boredom, I don't cause him distress. I don't promise anything, or give any advice based on my supposedly intuitive knowledge. I'm simply entertaining him. Giving just a little more bang for his buck, without actually providing any bang. Usually my clients are happy with the entertainment they receive, likely understanding it is just a game. Other than some sexual frustration and a mild case of buyer's remorse, I'm not doing him any real emotional harm.

Unfortunately, there are psychics and mediums out there who cause quite a lot of harm, and specifically prey on the grief stricken. You may have seen or read about psychics involved in criminal cases, or mediums providing messages from beyond the grave. These are the not-so-harmless types of con artists who use not only cold reading, but warm and hot readings as well. Warm and hot readings are much like their chilly counterparts except they use information secretly gathered about the subject before the reading. They also employ many other psychological tricks in order to make enormous amounts of money, all while claiming mystical powers. Mediums who prey on vulnerable people are, in my opinion, some of the worst people on the face of the planet.

When I was in culinary school, I was given a gift certificate for a psychic reading. I was, of course, skeptical, but what the hell, it was free, so I booked the appointment. When I walked through the beaded curtain into a plume of incense-polluted air, I was utterly un-amazed at the stereotypical décor. I was greeted by a kindly looking middle-aged woman who was dressed as expected. Having just come from class, I was exhausted from a day spent elbow deep in pastry flour and sugar. My reader invited me to have a seat and our session began.

She started by looking intensely into my eyes, which came off to me as much creepier than I expect she intended, but I resisted the urge to look away, refusing to be the first to break away from this weird game of eye chicken. I half expected her to move in for a kiss. She was not really my type. She then began to speak. She told me I was married. I was. She told me I wanted to have kids and would be pregnant at least three times, but that I would only have two live births – something I found rather morbid, actually. She said I was working toward a goal, and that I would be very successful in the career I chose. Then the real revelation came. She told me I had been a man in a past life and that was why I tended to be outspoken, stubborn and sometimes a little brash. As if only men could have those traits.

So, how accurate was this fortune teller? Well, although I wasn't wearing my wedding ring on my finger due to health regulations on food preparation, I was wearing it on a chain around my neck. I was also wearing my school chef's coat complete with my school's name on it. If she had meant that I would be successful as a chef, she was dead wrong. In fact, although I am a skilled pastry chef, my problems assimilating into an employee/employer relationship had prevented any success that I may have had in my chosen career. But she did say I was stubborn, outspoken, and brash and that would seem to be consistent with a problem with authority. Those traits were probably pretty apparent by my crossed arms and the return of her intense gaze. If I had met someone who was glaring at me like that, I might surmise they were stubborn and brash, also, maybe even just a little bitchy. Moving on, I did end up having a kid. Just one, and the result of just one pregnancy. I'm fixed now, which pretty much guarantees no more kids. Unless you count my cats, whom I often talk to like my children.

This so-called psychic was very obviously not psychic, and not even very good at pretending to be. I guess that would explain why the building she once occupied is now a payday loan office. Ironically, the new occupants of the building are probably much better at predicting the future, as they are very good at predicting which people will not be able to pay off their loans before accruing massive interest debt. But I digress. I was ultimately not very impressed by my first encounter with a psychic reader. She was also incorrect in predicting that I would be interested in further readings, as she insisted I take her card to schedule said future readings. Other than wasting the money of the friend who bought the gift certificate, this reading was harmless. Actually, it was kind of fun, so maybe not a total waste, as I was entertained. My second trip to a psychic was not so harmless and left me pretty pissed off.

My former bestie, Barbie, and I were at one time very experienced in the occult. Wait, what? That's right, one of our favorite pastimes involved such things as visiting reportedly haunted sites, playing around with crystals, and even a few Ouija board sessions. I have always harbored a love of ghost stories, horror books, and a taste for the macabre, so these topics naturally interested me. I can't say I believed in any of the stuff we looked at, but when paired with a few adult beverages, I found our research highly entertaining. Most of this stuff was ridiculous and easily debunked, although she took it a little more seriously than I did. I never had a real problem with any of it until she talked me into going to a medium.

About a year prior to my second and last visit to a psychic, Barbie had lost a child. Her baby girl had been born with a severe heart defect and passed away at five months old. Barbie had spent almost the entire five months in the hospital while her daughter underwent several open-heart surgeries. Unfortunately, before this, she had also suffered a miscarriage. Barbie had always wanted kids, so these two experiences left her understandably heartbroken and depressed. Her emotional state and the choices she made to cope with it were major factors in our friendship deteriorating. When she picked me up and told me she had booked a session for both of us with a psychic medium, I was very concerned and upset. I tried to get her to cancel, even promising to reimburse her for the money she had already spent, but my efforts were futile.

While she was knocking on the door to the psychic's residence/office, I was still trying to get her to turn around and leave. Barbie was just as stubborn as I was. My next best option I figured would be to try to protect her as best I could from what I suspected would turn out to be a con artist. The door opened, and we walked into a very normal looking foyer. There were two mediums waiting for us, as Barbie had booked a session for each of us. We were led into separate rooms with our respective charlatans. I was told that I had two child guardian angels around me. Irony seems to be a consistent theme in my limited experience with psychics, as I was told that one of the angels was a baby, likely a girl. I listened politely to several more mind-blowing revelations that were not so much mind blowing as they were just vaguely accurate, before insisting on checking on my friend.

She was a blubbering mess, something I had accurately predicted. She had expected to be told that her baby girl was with her and watching over her from heaven. She had instead been given a plethora of random statements that offered not even a small superficial amount of comfort. The whole experience exacerbated her grief and depression, and shockingly didn't dispel her belief in psychics in the slightest. When the psychic realized she had not performed as expected, she offered several lukewarm excuses as to why she hadn't been able to communicate with the child. Even stating that the child was too young to be heard from beyond the grave. Remember, in my reading I had been told all about a child spirit, so I guess Barbie just got the wrong medium.

The amount of anger I was left with after that encounter really changed the way I looked at this sort of harmless fun. Barbie continued on a self-destructive path after that, which involved several thousands of dollars spent in the hope she would eventually communicate with her daughter. I was not invited to these subsequent readings. I now look at mediums who tout their abilities to communicate with deceased loved ones as criminals, plain and simple. Really nothing more than con artists exploiting grief. Because our relationship ended, I don't know if Barbie ever really recovered emotionally from her loss, but I would be surprised if she did.

Grief sucks. Losing someone you love is in my experience one of the worst things you can go through. Unfortunately, this isn't the only experience I have with someone trying to cope with the crushing sense of grief using the paranormal or supernatural. My own family has been taken in by the hope of communicating with people who have passed away. There are several famous mediums who travel the country like rock stars perpetrating the same con. Just in case you can't make a live show, you can find a few on TV, duping celebrities and regular people alike. Disgusting. When a stripper is questioning your morals and ethics, I think you can safely assume that you are a first-rate asshole. Rant over. I hope you can understand my passionate objection to this kind of deceit and blatant exploitation of grief.

This and other experiences are part of what led me to the skeptical worldview I now hold. It is one thing to believe the magician can really make a rabbit materialize out of a hat obviously too small to hold such a thing, and another to believe that for a fee, someone can deliver a message from beyond the grave. One of those things is a benign form of entertainment, while the other is emotional abuse for profit.

Allowing a certain amount of magical thinking and mysticism in your life can be fun and entertaining. Maybe even important. Sometimes you can be too skeptical. I have ruined many a good horror movie by pointing out plot holes and implausible scenarios. Which, by the way, is a great way to end up watching horror movies alone. I have found that suspending critical thinking to obtain the thrill that comes with watching some poor sap run from a flesh-eating zombie is terribly entertaining. I would hate to have watched *Interview with a Vampire*, without being able to imagine for just a moment an eternity with a pale, long-haired Brad Pitt. Throw in a little Tom Cruise, Christian Slater, and a bit of Antonio Banderas, along with the idea that vampires are not susceptible to venereal diseases, and I am suddenly willing to suspend all critical thinking.

Don't be afraid to stick a quarter in Zoltar's magic fortune telling slot. Crack open that fortune cookie, and maybe even attend a séance if it strikes your fancy. Just be aware that while it may be fun to ponder these things, there is simply no empirical evidence that any of it is based in reality. Especially in times of grief or other hardship, relying on these kinds of cons for comfort can be detrimental to your health and wallet.

Chapter 15

You Look Like You Saw a Ghost

Wanting Something Does Not Make It Real

As I walk up the darkened staircase toward the dressing room, I feel the hairs on the back of my neck start to rise. The tiny lights that were intended to make this journey slightly less treacherous were failing miserably at their job. The hopelessly shaggy shag carpeting on the stairs is accentuating the fatigue I feel in my legs and feet. It's close to three a.m. and my vision is starting to blur, partly from my contacts which have started to feel like sandpaper and partly because of the Tequila Sunrises I was talked into drinking with my customer. It is not my usual modus operandi to drink at work, but in this case, I made an exception. This club was located right behind my hotel and security would walk me to my room. Not only would I not have to drive, but my customer would be with me until closing, so I wouldn't really have to work, either.

I felt like I had just run a marathon. A naked marathon which mostly involved dodging lips and tongue intent on making contact with my breasts. Unfortunately, in my exhaustion, I miscalculated a move, and was duly rewarded with a sloppy wet kiss on my cheek, reminding me why I don't drink at work. There were still a few hours left before I would retreat to my hotel room, and a short break and a fresh piece of gum would help me make it through the rest of the night.

As I neared the landing at the top of the stairs, I was slightly troubled by the lack of noise coming from the dressing room. At this time of the night, I knew that most of the girls were downstairs draining shot glasses and wallets. This was prime lap dancing time,

125

but I did expect to hear at least one or two girls upstairs. The dressing room doorway is to the left of the landing. I turn to enter. I walk into the room still filled with lingering cigarette smoke as was the rest of the club, and sense something odd. I see a shadow out of the corner of my eye and turn toward it, expecting to see another dancer. What greeted me instead was a dark figure near the ceiling. In a fraction of a second, I saw a man-shaped thing hanging from a noose tied to the rafters. His head slightly bent and tongue lolling out of his mouth. It should be much too dark to make out his eyes, and yet I can see them staring at me, a horrifying glowing yellow. He didn't blink, only stared at me in a threatening manner that turned my stomach into glass. Panic left me frozen in place. My vision doubled, and I blinked involuntarily. When I opened my eyes, the putrid hanging man was gone.

I quickly retreated back downstairs to the main floor of the club. The DJ had gum, why bother with opening my locker anyway? Plus, my fatigue had been conveniently replaced with an ample amount of adrenaline. I wasn't so tired anymore. I made a stop at the DJ booth, where he took one look at me and said, "You look like you've just seen a ghost."

I replied with a smirk, "No, I'm always this pale." I procured my gum and took a seat at the bar where I asked for a glass of water. As I sipped, my heartrate started to return to normal and I thought about what I had just experienced.

The building located in downtown Reno, Nevada, which now housed a strip club, had at one time been a slaughterhouse. While I have never been able to verify if that was historically true, the persistent odor seemed consistent with the story. It had been said that there was a worker who had hung himself in the breakroom shortly before the slaughterhouse went out of business – the very breakroom which now served as the dressing room for the current topless dancers. The building itself was creepy enough without the accompanying back story. It was kind of off the beaten path as strip clubs usually are and was typically dark and dingy. This particular club catered mostly to the blue-collar type customer much like the ill-fated man who supposedly committed suicide there. When I heard the story, I couldn't help myself from wondering why he would want to keep hanging from the rafters in the dressing room, when he could've been downstairs discreetly ogling the topless dancers. Contrary to popular belief, what goes on in strip club dressing rooms is not usually that sexy, in fact most of the time it's pretty gross. I mean, if you got to be a ghost, why not make the best of it?

The ghost story was pretty popular with the girls here. The fun part, of course, was watching the expressions on the face of each new girl as the story was told. Always slightly different, depending on who was telling it, the story itself was scary, and eyewitnesses to the hanging ghost were always compelling. If so many people had seen the same thing, there had to be something to it, right? I definitely thought so. For the most part, we know better than to rely solely on people's memory, but when several people report seeing the same thing, it gives more validation to the claims. After all, I had witnessed pretty much the same thing as what had been told to me. The whole reason I had noticed the quiet before I entered the dressing room was because most girls simply refused to be up there alone.

The hanging man wasn't the only phenomena that was reported in the club, either. Footsteps, unexplained creaking sounds, and things being moved around were also commonly witnessed. Almost everyone who had heard the story also sensed a presence when alone and felt cold drafts at odd times. Finding someone who hadn't felt, seen, or heard something strange was much less common than someone who had. It seemed that the only people who didn't experience something weird in the club were people who hadn't heard of the story.

Ghost Hunting

In almost two decades as an exotic dancer I have worked in approximately twenty strip clubs in four states, and almost every single one has a ghost story. Lockers slamming, strange sounds, apparition sightings and the like. It is far rarer in my experience to find a club or even just an old building without some sort of paranormal ghostly background. It seems that the anomaly is the club, old house, or hotel that doesn't have a ghost story attached to it. Given my proclivity to ghost and horror stories, I have spent a good amount of my time researching and visiting such sites. Almost all of my ghost hunting excursions involve my ill-fated friendship with Barbie, although my interest in the subject started well before I met her.

When I was nine years old, my mom and I moved out of our suburban home in Southern California to a very small town in Northern California, right in the heart of gold country. When gold was first discovered in California in 1848, prompting the gold rush of 1849, the hills of Northern California were largely untamed. People from the East rushed to make their fortunes, but the vast majority of them were unsuccessful. The people who actually got rich from the gold rush were the merchants, bankers, and the like. As you might imagine, a lot of misery and death resulted. Murders, prostitution, and the indentured servitude of Chinese immigrants made for a whole hell of a lot of ghost stories.

As a kid, I was thoroughly surprised to learn that history held much more interest for me than Disneyland ever could. I went through a bit of a culture shock after we moved, when I realized that the mall was at least an hour and a half away and sidewalks were considered a luxury for *city folk*, but my fascination for the history of the place softened the blow a bit. Because my mom was a folk musician, I had access to many places that other people didn't. Shortly after moving there, my mom established a network of historians, museum docents, and artists who were all involved with the gold rush tourist industry. She played her music in historic estates that had been converted to bed and breakfasts, the Gold Rush museum, elementary schools, and many local events. In many of these places, she experienced her own unexplained occurrences. She reported that even though she always tuned her instruments before a performance, sometimes she would start to play only to discover her instruments would be suddenly out of tune. She also said she would feel or sense things that made her uncomfortable in a lot of these places.

The most memorable place, and one which she would complain the most about when she booked it, was an old estate called the Vineyard House. It is now unfortunately closed to the public, but at one time, it hosted tours and had a very decent restaurant where my mom would play for the dinner crowd. The Vineyard House, named for the vineyard and wine making operation it was originally intended to be, was a sprawling estate that included slave quarters, which, while extremely creepy, were not nearly as creepy as the basement where the wine was made. The man of the house apparently contracted syphilis from one of the many prostitutes who lived nearby, and after the disease progressed, was chained to a stone wall in the basement. When I toured the place as a kid, the shackles were still hanging there. Fun. One of the most reported phenomena was to hear him screaming and rattling his chains. Right across the road was the cemetery which also had a plethora of ghost stories and sightings. Barbie and I visited this particular cemetery many times at dusk, prime ghost sighting time.

My very first job in fact, was with a sandwich shop that was in one of the oldest houses right in the middle of Gold Discovery Park, located very close to the Vineyard House. It, too, had a very creepy basement. That basement, also supposed to be haunted, only held a large freezer where we kept the ice cream and other supplies. Thankfully, no shackles on the wall. Whenever I had to go down there for supplies, I would run half terrified back up to the main house, despite never having actually experienced anything worth running from.

When I met Barbie shortly after beginning my adventures as a nude entertainer, our mutual interest in morbid history helped cement our bond. We proceeded to venture to every haunted cemetery, hotel, and building within a hundred-mile radius of the little gold rush town. We researched the history as well as the ghost stories related to each place. When she suggested we take a trip to New Orleans, I knew her interest in that particular city was mostly in its ghost stories. New Orleans, in that respect, didn't disappoint, and actually didn't disappoint in almost every other respect, also, with the very notable exception of the public bathrooms on Bourbon Street, which were definitely haunted by some very earthly horrors.

Our main hotel was in a small town outside of New Orleans called Metairie. The La Quinta located in Metairie was much cheaper than staying in New Orleans itself. Since we got off the plane with only enough money for dinner that night and a two-week hotel stay, we went straight to Bourbon Street to look for a club to work in. We found one quickly and discovered that the staff there was just as excited to have two young dancers from California as we were to finally see some ghosts. The club we had chosen right on Bourbon Street had once been a brothel, so we were obviously delighted to find out that we would be working with a few ghost hookers. Thankfully, they didn't turn out to be much competition.

During our stay, we only worked about five nights. The rest of the time was spent ghost hunting and enjoying the various vomit-inducing beverages on the famed Bourbon Street. Because we were so well received at the club we chose, we were able to afford one night at one of the most haunted hotels in New Orleans. It had been a children's hospital that had burned down and been rebuilt. When they restored the building, the floors were rebuilt slightly higher than the original ones, which resulted in the apparitions being sighted from the shins up. I guess they didn't get the memo and were still walking around on the original levels.

We were incredibly excited for our stay. So much, in fact, that we bought a Ouija board for the occasion. At this point, we had been avid ghost hunters for about ten years but had yet to see a ghost. There had been many scary sounds and creepy feelings. We had definitely scared the shit out of each other, but really hadn't come away with any empirical evidence other than a few ghost orb pictures taken with disposable cameras. This was our chance. We were not disappointed.

The hotel was fairly close to Bourbon Street, so obviously we spent the first part of the evening getting properly lubricated for our stay in the ghost-ridden hotel. We were convinced that this would be it, we would finally get to see a real live ghost. Given the horrific nature of the place, and the fact that it had so many sightings, we knew it would be more likely than not that we would see a ghost. The tour guide who told us about the place practically guaranteed it. By the time we stumbled back to our rooms, we were primed and ready.

We opened the door to our room with our old-fashioned metal key. It groaned just like an old haunted door was supposed to. I took a brief moment in the bathroom to let go of the excess alcohol I drank before settling down on the floor with Barbie. She had set up the Ouija board and was eager to get started. We had used a Ouija board one other time in her parents' haunted cabin by Donner Lake, a place with its own super gross ghost stories – look up the Donner Party if you think you have the appetite for it, pun intended –

ultimately never really confirming whether or not we had contacted anything other than our drunk selves.

This time felt different, however. I mean, it was New Orleans after all, land of the voodoo. We placed our fingers on the planchette and both started to shiver at the same time. The little plastic triangle began to move slightly at first, then began to move in a circle. My heart started to race and once again I ran to the bathroom to let go of some of Louisiana's finest generic gin. I got back and placed my hands back on the planchette, which immediately started moving again, this time more aggressively. It started to spell something out. Y-O-U-W-I-L-L-D-I-E-T-O-N-I-T-E. It would seem that ghosts are not concerned with correct spelling, but whatever, we were going to die.

We freaked out, threw the Ouija board out the window, prompting a call from the manager with a stern warning. We dived into our respective beds. I took one more pit stop in the bathroom to throw up again, then proceeded to listen to the never-ending creaks and groans of the old hotel until the sun came up. I couldn't tell you if either one of us actually slept. When morning finally arrived, we could hardly wait to get back to the La Quinta to try to make sense of what we had witnessed. Curiously, we didn't die.

Not So Paranormal Revelation

Despite being scared shitless on multiple occasions, I have never seen a ghost. I've never actually seen or heard anything that couldn't ultimately be explained by something super normal. I have felt plenty of things but have yet to find an outside source for those feelings. I have been told you won't see a ghost if you are looking for it. OK, but that puts kind of a damper on all the ghost hunting reality shows. They seem to see stuff all the time. I have also been told that if you don't believe in ghosts or aren't receptive to them you won't see one either. I have been in both haunted places where I wasn't looking and places where I have, and nothing. After fifteen years of research with active and passive ghost hunting, I've come up with exactly zilch in the evidence for ghosts. I have however come across explanations for the vast majority of supposedly unexplainable phenomenon. But what about the hanging slaughterhouse guy? Well, I'm glad you asked.

Let's revisit the situation. The dark staircase leading up to the dressing room set the stage, it was creepy. I was exhausted both physically and mentally, throw in some high-end tequila, a scary story, a set of disposable contacts which were ready to be disposed of, and I was ready to see a ghost. By the time I sat down at the bar, I had already started to realize that I hadn't really seen anything at all. And on my next trip up to Reno, I had the chance to hear someone repeating the story to an enthralled new girl. As I listened, I noticed that the details about the ghost's clothing and where he was usually sighted didn't line up with what I thought I saw. This gave me the last bit of confirmation that what I saw came from my weary imagination, and to be fair, the booze.

But the Ouija board? Like the previous situation, alcohol was involved, so was fatigue. Ouija boards have been investigated extensively and it has been shown that they involve our own involuntary micro movements to move the planchette. Barbie and I were drunk and already primed to scare ourselves silly. We did just that. The set-up at her family's cabin was much the same. It is not a coincidence that most ghost sightings happen around three a.m. Sleep deprivation causes the brain to do some weird stuff. Our brains are highly suggestible, which makes us really easy to fool, especially when we're tired.

At the time that most ghosts are sighted, our brains are usually primed for sleep, and not just to sleep, but to dream. Before we actually fall asleep, our brains will go into a state that is between waking and sleeping. In that state, we are getting ready to dream, and even more suggestible than when we are fully awake. A year after my mom passed, as I was falling asleep, I distinctly heard her call my name. I sat up and took a moment to process what had happened. It was her voice and it sounded like it came from just outside my room. Me, being the hopeless skeptic, did just a little research and found this was a common grief hallucination. To hear a passed loved one's voice is very common, and almost always happens when someone is in bed. One of the things I have struggled with after losing my mom was feeling like her memory was fading. Hearing her call my name so clearly reinforced the memory of her voice. I actually found some comfort in it, despite understanding that it came from my own brain. It was like finding a hidden recording. No matter where it came from, I got to hear her call my name.

There are cases where people report being held down by a ghost while they are in bed. Sometimes referred to as an old hag or night hag, it is when someone sees or feels a ghost sitting on them making them unable to move or scream. This happens either when someone is woken up or when they are falling asleep and is called sleep paralysis. When your brain goes to sleep, there is a part of it that is supposed to turn off the mechanism that makes your body move. That is to prevent you from physically acting out your dreams. This mechanism can malfunction. When these malfunctions occur, some crazy shit happens. You can be sort of awake but can't move. Or in the case of a sleepwalker, sleeping but walking around scaring the shit out of people you live with. My husband and kid have both walked around in their sleep, and it's pretty freaky. I have had an old hag-like dream when I was a teenager, except it was a man holding me down. It was one of the scariest things I have been through. I can understand why people going through it would be utterly terrified and simultaneously convinced it was something paranormal. It absolutely feels real.

Memories also play a huge part in ghost sightings. It isn't just cognitive biases and anxious reactions that cloud our perception of reality. Our memories can also be a pain in the ass. When we remember something, our brain will recreate the event, and a good portion of the time alter it to fit our biases or even other peoples' depictions of the event. Have you ever gotten into an argument with someone over the details of a shared event? Maybe found it super weird that they remembered it totally different than you did? That is a product of our flawed human memory. Our brains are forever changing our perception to fit whatever narrative it likes better, even if not accurate. It is the prime reason why eyewitness testimony is not considered the most reliable evidence in court.

As far as ghost orbs, and other photographic evidence, well, that is almost always found to be a light or camera issue. Not very convincing evidence if you look into it. With photo and video manipulation software so easy to use and readily available, photographic evidence becomes even more unreliable. Weird sounds, sightings, and feelings are all also not very convincing if you start to look for a source. My mom's instruments mysteriously going out of tune is easily explained by elevation, humidity, and temperature changes. There are things that have gone unexplained, but just because you can't find an explanation for something doesn't mean it doesn't have one, or that it comes from a paranormal or supernatural source. My husband, in fact, has a couple very compelling ghost stories, but even he admits they could've probably been explained had they been investigated at the time they happened.

Despite all the debunking of hauntings and such, ghost stories have not lost much of their appeal for me. I still enjoy a good scare and am still susceptible to freaking out just a little. One night a few years ago, I was lying on my bed watching a show on TV about hauntings. My son was asleep in his room, and my husband was out of town. My elderly cat was softly snoring on the end of my bed, when he suddenly woke up and looked alarmed. My other cat started howling as he walked toward my room down the hallway as that was happening. I felt the bed start to rock underneath me. Adrenaline surged through my body. I was afraid to move, and then it all stopped. Both cats still seemed on edge but were settling down, I wasn't sure what to do at that point. I was trying desperately to convince myself that a ghost had not just been softly rocking my bed. I lay there for a moment, trying to calm down. I figured I'd distract myself and check out my Facebook feed. The first post was someone asking about the earthquake that had just happened.

In Southern California I had been through several large earthquakes. Noisy, rolling, and utterly disconcerting. My experience with earthquakes was that they weren't gentle in the slightest. I was also under the false impression that we didn't have them so far inland in Northern California. I had just experienced the wimpiest of all earthquakes, and it nearly gave me a heart attack. Stupid haunting show. Even the knowledge that ghosts aren't real didn't inoculate me from scaring myself half to death. My cat even looked at me like I was an idiot, although he always looks at me like that.

Understanding the reality of the phenomena hasn't detracted at all from the entertainment aspect for me. I think it is a great demonstration of how a balance between skepticism and mystery can be fostered. Pondering the things we don't have explanations for can be really fun and can lead to discovering things about our world we didn't know or understand. When you investigate this kind of stuff you can learn a lot about the world and how it works, but also about yourself. The history of the people who end up in ghost stories tells us much more about the living than the dead. It isn't so hard to relate to a lot of them, and that gives us a chance to take a deeper look at our own lives.

Ghost stories are ultimately human stories. All the really good ghost stories involve some tragedy or some unfinished business. A love story gone south, or a missed opportunity that is now being pursued beyond the grave. These stories give us an opportunity to consider our own stories and what we could be missing in our own lives. They present, in many instances, cautionary tales that may lead us to take those chances or make changes to our current circumstances that we may not have considered before. It may seem like the tales of hauntings are about death, but I don't think that is the case at all. If looked at from this perspective, ghosts are more about life before death rather than after it. After all, who wants to be the ghost wallowing in regrets, hanging from the rafters in a strip club?

Chapter 16

Strippers Exposed

Build Your Own Bullshit Detector

When I started writing my first book in 2012, I was a little apprehensive writing about the adult entertainment industry. While it's true that I was annoyed by the misconceptions and stereotypes that existed in the mainstream media, I wasn't sure if I actually had the balls to write the truth as I know it. When I mentioned the idea to several colleagues, I got some push back and even a few warnings. At one point I was even threatened about exposing some of the darker sides of the adult entertainment industry. Yes, I know most of the other books about stripping talk about prostitution, rampant drug use, and abuse by staff and partners of strippers and other dark stuff, but the actual truth is much darker. Honestly, I was afraid to tell it.

In the end, I decided that I would write about my own life in the industry. I figured I would simply offer a counter argument to the stereotypical depiction of strippers that was currently out there. I changed all the names except mine in an effort to appear to be protecting those who might be embarrassed by my stories. I also changed the names of the clubs so that it looked like I was really exposing secrets that the clubs wouldn't want out there. In essence, I wimped out. I gave in to the pressure to keep quiet. In this book, this chapter, I have decided to tell the real truth about the adult entertainment industry and the people involved. It is far scarier than you could ever imagine.

This is going to sound crazy, and perhaps it is, but strippers have been involved in almost every major effort to repress the sexual revolution since the 1960s. In some cases, disposing of *problem* informants. You read that correctly, strippers and those involved in the industry have been involved in an extensive coordinated effort to demonize sex and stripping in mainstream society. Getting that off my chest is a huge relief, although I expect the backlash to be equally huge. All of the books and talk shows that talk about how damaging the sex industry is to women and men and even society as a whole, have been carefully orchestrated by the very people they are meant to disparage. While you let that fact sink in, let me give you a little history lesson on the origins of stripping.

The first time a woman was said to be compensated for dancing provocatively actually dates back to the bible. The daughter of the Jewish princess Herodias performed the Dance of the Seven Veils for King Herod for his birthday celebration. He was so impressed, I think we can safely assume he got a boner, that he granted her request for John the Baptist's Head on a platter. I, for one, am really grateful that dollar bills are now the accepted form of payment.

The art of sexual exotic dancing itself goes back way farther than that. Evidence of seductive dancing can be found in Paleolithic cave paintings in the south of France from twenty thousand years ago. There have been statuettes of exotic dancers found near the Black Sea regions of Bulgaria and Romania that are estimated to be over nine thousand years old. In Greek and Roman times, erotic dancers performed in sacred temples to honor the moon, the hunt, and the god of wine, as well as other ritualistic purposes.

In the 14th century, belly dancing was invented in the Middle East. While they kept their clothes on, the movements are obviously sexual in nature. This is when the money really entered the scene. The audience would toss coins at the dancers to show their appreciation. Just so there is no confusion, tossing quarters or other coins at modern strippers is frowned upon, and will likely result in your being escorted out of the club by a large bouncer. Erotic dancing was also common in the temples of India in the form of sacred rituals. The fact that exotic dances have been performed as part of religious ceremonies is really important, so keep that in mind.

Eighteenth century Britain is where the art of stripping really started to take off. Burlesque shows involved a lot of theatrics, parody, and music. When it became apparent that the sexual aspect of these shows was the main draw, the striptease was invented and brought to America. Striptease and pole dancing started in the 1920s, performed in side show tents at the traveling fairs. In the 1950s they moved from tents to bars. This was really the beginning of the modern strip club as we know it today. Back then, strip clubs were often raided, and shut down in an effort to conserve wholesome values. Like the prohibition of alcohol, it had the opposite effect. Then came the sexual revolution in the 1960s, and this is where things get a little sketchy.

While it may seem like free love and open sexual expression would be a great thing for strippers, it wasn't. Just like the legalization of alcohol hurt the moonshine business, the idea that sex would become normal, even accepted in polite society, was a huge threat to strippers. If nudity were to become mainstream, there would be a lot of ass shakers who would have to get real jobs. Or even worse, become subservient housewives. The very lucrative business of manipulating horny men would be destroyed. Like a lot of industries that are threatened by progress, the strip clubs had to find a way to combat this new push toward the acceptance of sexuality.

Religion and conservative politics became the perfect cover for protecting the livelihood of exotic dancers. I know it seems nuts, but the fact that misogyny is so rampant in religious texts and its respective dogma made it a perfect vehicle to combat the hippies burning their bras. The whole underground secret maneuvering actually started in San Francisco in late 1969 with a few strip club owners, and still operates today. While only a few dancers are involved, there are a good many who meet in secret once a year to set the agenda.

Here is where the real risk I'm taking in writing this becomes apparent. Before retiring, I was one of the dancers who personally witnessed the coordination and development of that agenda. When I lived in Las Vegas, I attended one of these conferences. They are usually scheduled in late January to coincide with the Adult Entertainment Awards. This is a huge event and provides a good cover for the owners and stripper operatives in Las

Vegas. Also, January is usually a slower time for strip clubs in general. After the Christmas holiday spending binge and before people start to get their tax refunds, it is the perfect time to take a break from the club. I learned about these meetings from a friend of mine who is fairly high up in the ranks who was invited to attend. She thought I could be helpful to the cause because of my Catholic background. The strippers who are a part of all this, act as intel gatherers. Because they are on the front lines, so to speak, the entertainers can gain all sorts of information helpful to the clandestine efforts. Guys with hard-ons are pretty easy to get information out of.

I was surprised to learn that most of the actual operatives were not strippers themselves. They are older men and women who have placed themselves high up in political and religious movements. You've heard of some if not all of them. I won't repeat their names here for legal and personal safety reasons. They are the people who speak against sexual expression in all its forms. They push legislation and policies that speak to the immorality of public nudity. The pearl clutchers, and pious conservatives who seem intensely sexually repressed. They frown upon any and all open sexual expression and are great at keeping up appearances, but in reality, are usually quite perverse. In fact, a few of the prominent conservative activists who get caught doing dirty shit are actually involved in the scheme. Remember Jim Bakker? There's a reason Tammy wore so much damn make up. Very few people knew she was actually a very popular stripper in her time, went by the name of Chastity. Jim himself was adamant in advocating the demonization of sex. Until he got a little too greedy of course and got caught.

Strip club owners are funding the effort for obvious reasons. Because strip clubs deal mostly in cash, it is a great way to grease the political wheels outside of the official books. Strip clubs function much like mafia run businesses, and the money flows like glitter. I'm fairly certain that there are several well-known and not so well-known mafia members involved as well. I have known loose lipped strippers who have stumbled on some of this activity and, well, I'm fairly certain they're now chilling with Jimmy Hoffa, wherever he ended up. Swimming with the fishes, if you catch my drift. Now you may have a better understanding of why I was afraid

140

to speak up. Writing about boners in sweatpants, was simply much safer.

There are two reasons why I'm choosing to talk now. The first is that I'm no longer in the business and the risk is slightly less. The second and main reason is, the efforts to push religion in government are ramping up. With music and media becoming more and more sexually graphic, the efforts of this dark stripper illuminati are becoming more brazen. As sex and nudity become more acceptable, society is starting to see that the shame and guilt that religion attaches to sex is bullshit. Strip club owners and some dancers are drastically escalating their efforts. There is a disproportionate number of religious people controlling our government. There are bills right now trying to get the bible taught in classrooms. These bills are designed to create more strippers and strip club customers. They understand that the more they make sex seem dirty, the more people will be drawn to strip clubs as well as other facets of the sex industry. It is simple biology, which is why science is being demonized as well. Take away the guilt and shame, and the strip clubs go away, too. The threat my friends, is very real.

Down the Rabbit Hole of Bullshit

Much of what I wrote above is complete and utter bullshit. There are factual components, but the premise itself is garbage. And yet, when I repeated the lie to several people who would know better, they bought into it completely. In one case, they were really surprised that I was just telling them about it now. Is it really that far-fetched to think that Tammy Faye Bakker might have been a stripper at one point? I'm not even trying to be mean, but come on, porn stars wear less makeup.

Just so there is no mistake, there is no conspiracy of strip club owners pushing a political or religious sexual repression agenda in order to make the sex industry more lucrative. That also means they are not murdering people who talk about it. The history of erotic dancing that I just shared is very true, as well as very interesting, in my opinion. The adult entertainment award event is another real thing. I offered the stripper illuminati example as a way to show how easy it is to create a conspiracy where there is none. Weaving a few known true facts in with abject lies is the most effective way to build a conspiracy theory.

As a dancer, I have fallen prey many times to conspiracy type thinking. Because my money and validation depends so much on my looks, it is really hard to not look for some sort of explanation for a bad night other than I'm simply not good enough. In trying to protect my fragile self-esteem, I have absolutely placed the blame on anything or anybody other than myself. That led to a whole lot of *someone is out to get me* type thinking. Stripper paranoia if you will. As rational as I think I am, I have wasted a good amount of time wondering who is doing things I can't compete with. Or maybe someone is talking about me to customers, thus adversely affecting my money. The human brain can come up with all sorts of crazy ideas to protect itself from any information that may not be consistent with our egos or whatever it is we want to be true. As a dancer, trying to parse the truth from reality can be extremely difficult sometimes.

I can take some comfort in the fact that I am not the only stripper to invent conspiracy narratives about their coworkers. I was only nineteen when I made the harrowing trip to Reno to dance for the first time. It was a high-end club, who catered mostly to white collar businessmen. As a rookie stripper, it was hugely intimidating, and I had yet to establish any type of reputation there. Because I was pretty much terrified of the other dancers, I tried to keep a low profile. My efforts soon proved futile because shortly after stepping on to the floor for the first time, I caught the attention of the two main house girls. These girls, or women, I should say, were like the alpha strippers who went by the names of Naughty and Nice. They were ancient from my late teenage perspective, so they were probably around twenty-eight or so.

Naughty and Nice were impressive. They had a spectacular dance routine set to Falco's *Rock Me Amadeus* that included elaborate costumes complete with powdered wigs. I was absolutely awestruck and petrified of them at the same time. I was under the impression that they had not noticed me, until Naughty decided to abruptly shatter my false sense of security. I was sitting with a nicely dressed businessman, trying to figure out how to ask him to go to the VIP room. I hadn't yet developed the skills to accomplish this without being super awkward, so I was horrified when Naughty unceremoniously sat on his lap. Talking to a customer when another girl is talking to him is one of the most egregious violations of dancer etiquette. But, in my naiveté, I had no idea how to handle the situation. I just sat there and smiled stupidly while she giggled and flirted with him. He had put a hundred-dollar bill on the table right before she sat down. I had been hoping it was for me. Naughty put her hand on the bill and said, "Is this for me?"

To which he replied, "No, it's for her," and slid the bill from under her hand. Naughty was obviously pissed but said nothing and walked away in a huff. He then handed me the bill and asked to go to the VIP where he proceeded to spend a good amount of time and money on me. I was only temporarily relieved. I mistakenly thought that Naughty had been put in her place and would leave me alone. It turns out that I had become the target of a newly contrived and vindictive stripper conspiracy. I was apparently fucking the owner of the club and was a meth head as well. Spoiler alert: I had never met the owner and would've been surprised if he had any idea who I was. I am also pretty high-strung naturally, so meth wouldn't be a likely drug of choice for me.

That was unfortunately not the end of the rumors and conspiracies spread by Naughty and Nice. Nice, by the way, was just as mean as Naughty. Unbeknownst to me, I was fucking and giving blow jobs to every guy who walked in the door, including the maintenance men. At least I was generous. Eventually, the truth proved unavoidable. There was simply no supporting evidence to their claims, and they ended up looking like the assholes they were. The fact that I was skinny and scantily dressed was the only evidence they had to prove that I was sleeping with the owner and doing speed. Neither of those things held up to any kind of scrutiny when pressed, so it became pretty obvious that they were making shit up.

I wish I could say that I learned not to do the same thing they did from that experience, but that would be untrue. Time and time again, I resorted to the same type of thinking when I felt like my self-esteem was threatened. I semi-convinced myself on several occasions that there were people actively sabotaging my income. What I ultimately came to understand was that the only person sabotaging me was me. By giving in to the need to build a cover story for why I wasn't doing well, I made myself look like the asshole. In trying to hide my insecurities, I made them much more obvious and ended up adversely affecting my own money.

This became clear to me when I listened to a friend of mine talk about how one of the new girls was probably giving head in the VIP room. I finally understood how this type of stripper conspiracy thinking was counterproductive. It was a hard habit to break, but by hearing someone else spin a web of garbage to justify why she wasn't making the money she thought she should be, I recognized the flaw in my own thinking. When I stopped trying to come up with reasons why someone else might be doing better than me, I started making money. When I focused on myself, I was able to progress and let go of the resentment and jealousy that was leading me to make up stories about my competition.

Climbing Out of the Rabbit Hole

Conspiracies are just another example of human beings trying to explain things they don't have answers for. Sometimes conspiracies are a way to sell things or push an ideology, or sometimes just to pass the time. Our brains are, for the most part, not satisfied with not knowing how things work, or with an answer that seems too simple. When I was a kid, I had a book of unsolved mysteries that included a lengthy chapter on crop circles. The evidence was laid out meticulously. I was convinced they were made by aliens. I entertained the idea that they were man made at first, but when I read the so-called evidence stating the crop circles were too complicated to be made by humans was presented to me in a certain way, I believed it. The idea that someone would take that amount of time and effort to perpetrate a hoax seemed ridiculous. My brain didn't want to accept the simplest explanation, it wanted something more elaborate and exciting. Aliens were definitely more exciting than some dude with a wooden plank, a rope, and way too much time on his hands.

Just as we can believe conspiracies presented by other people, we can also unknowingly create our own conspiracy theories to explain things in our own lives. Plenty of smart people fall victim to conspiracies, but when critical thinking and fact checking factor in, they are usually able to see where they have been duped. There are several ways to find out if, say, a race of lizard people is masquerading as world leaders and is plotting to destroy the earth. The first is: People are really terrible at keeping secrets. Benjamin Franklin is quoted as saying, "Three may keep a secret, if two of them are dead." The chances of someone not blabbing about some salacious event is almost zero. If no one has leaked actual evidence about a particular conspiracy, it is likely garbage. Someone would have provided some proof of lizard people by now.

Another way to tell if a conspiracy theory has any truth to it is the available evidence. Real conspiracies such as Watergate had an extensive money trail and recordings which proved it to be true. While bullshit conspiracy theories are made up of subjective speculation, misunderstood science, or alleged evidence, when pressed, there is no substance to back up extraordinary claims. Conspiracy theorists will also point to proven conspiracies and say look, that one was real, so this one could be, too. Just because Nixon really was a crook doesn't automatically mean that Elvis is still alive. A common argument is that the people behind the conspiracy are so intelligent and skilled as to not have left a shred of evidence behind. That's why it hasn't been uncovered, duh. Except, of course, for the person making the allegations. Apparently, the conspirators are exceptionally skilled at hiding evidence from everyone except the random guy on the internet.

Conspiracies are often constructed to explain otherwise mundane anomalies. Oftentimes, the goal of the conspiracy simply doesn't justify the method. The flat earth conspiracy is an example of the method not fitting the goal. While they may be able to invent some bizarre *scientific facts* to justify their position, the whole thing falls apart when you ask why the government wants us to think the earth is round. Really, what is the point? Who benefits from convincing the population that the earth is really round and not flat? No one. However, there are many who benefit from convincing gullible people that the earth is flat. The people pushing this theory want attention, they want to feel like they belong to a community, and so they are mostly doing it to gain followers on social media.

While strippers may weave tales to protect their egos, the need to feel accepted and part of a group is another reason people want to engage in pushing conspiracy theories. When you feel like you are the only people out there who know the *truth* it can help you feel like you belong. Like you are part of some chat room clique, you and your fellow keyboard warriors are the smart ones who figured it all out, just waiting for the rest of the world to catch up. As comforting as it may be to feel like you know better than everyone else, it can be dangerous to get caught up in conspiracy theories. Unfortunately, there have been some less than stable people who have acted on theories they have been convinced of. When people fall too far down the rabbit hole of a conspiracy theory it can have major consequences.

Conspiracies can be entertaining. Sometimes imagining some deeper meaning or cause to things that have otherwise normal answers is simply fun. Like other types of magical thinking, you can take it too far. The temptation to spread a conspiracy theory can be hard to resist, the look on someone's face when you tell them that strippers and strip club owners are trying to sabotage healthy sexual expression is humorous for sure. Knowing when to quit and accept that the most mundane explanation for an unusual or suspicious event is important to know. If you're not careful, conspiracy thinking can snowball. Suddenly there may be lizard people everywhere.

With so much disinformation out there in the world it can be easy to get caught up in some of these theories, even if you are smart and know how to fact check. Fear and insecurity can be a powerful driving force in our lives and can lead us to believe some stuff that isn't true. If you can realize where your fear and insecurity are driving you to believe or make up things that have no substance, you will have created a natural defense against conspiracy thinking. There are enough real things to fear in the world without having to worry if your microwave is spying on you. If you read or hear something that strikes fear in you, take a deep breath, do a little fact checking, and relax. It is far more likely than not that what is being presented might just be a conspiracy theory designed to scare you. While there is power in fear, there is a greater power in knowing just what is worth being afraid of.

Chapter 17

Trust Me, I'm Not a Doctor

Outsmart the Alluring Spokesperson

There are many perks that come with being a stripper. For instance, when an establishment I worked for partnered with a local radio station, I was chosen to help promote the club. In return, I went to many concerts for free, got a ton of t-shirts and other swag, and was lucky enough to be chosen to wrestle in Lucky Charms on St. Patrick's Day. I'm on the fence as to whether to consider the latter as a perk because it was super gross. I had my face dunked in melted marshmallows and reconstituted powdered milk. There are other perks as well. Strippers get discounts sometimes at local businesses that sell costumes and other stripper gear. Costumes being a bit of a misnomer if you ask me, since it's not like we're hiding much.

We also have access to free professional advice. Like the lawyer in Vegas who explained to me how to win a judgement against an unscrupulous landlord, or the financial advisor who told me to never take advice from a financial advisor. There was the pharmaceutical lobbyist who unintentionally gave me information as to how the future opioid problem would start, bragging about his sales pitch to doctors. Strippers tend to meet a lot of doctors as well. I met an optometrist who let me in on the disposable contact racket, saving me quite a lot of money. When meeting these types of professionals in the strip club setting, you can learn a lot that the general public may not get to hear for free. I may have mentioned this earlier, but boobs and booze make guys talk, like a sexual truth serum.

I tend to trust what I hear from these guys because they are paying me, not the other way around. They simply don't have any financial motivation to lie to me. The only reason a customer may lie to me would be to impress me, like the guy who told me we could travel the world because he was El Chapo's nephew. I was not impressed, by the way. I told him, "Sure, we could travel the world on the cartel's money, then retire in a sunny ditch somewhere *sans* heads." That guy was likely lying. At least, I hope he was. But for the most part, I believe the professionals who tell me about their respective industries.

In the early 2000s I was working at a topless bar which happened to be located next to a chiropractic office. Dr. Bob was a frequent patron of the bar. I talked with him often, but never lap danced for him. He would tip occasionally on stage. I liked Dr. Bob, so when one day he noticed me rubbing my back and offered an exam at his office, I accepted. Usually, I don't see any customer outside of the club, but Dr. Bob was not only a Dr. but everyone knew him at the club. He had treated other dancers, staff, and I think even the owner. I had good reason to not be as cautious around him as I would with other customers. Plus, none of the other girls said he was weird when he was alone with them in his office.

His office was normal, and the exam professional. I had to hand it to him, despite eyeballing my boobs at least twice a week, he was very respectful. Had I not known him from the club, I wouldn't have guessed by his exam that he went to strip clubs at all. No wandering hands or creepy comments. His bedside manner was impeccable. His diagnosis seemed on the mark, too. My spine was out of alignment, causing my lower back pain. The super high heels were the likely culprit. He described his treatment plan, and we worked out an affordable payment and treatment schedule. He even gave me a free adjustment on my first visit. It didn't help much, but that was because it would take multiple treatments to fix my problem, he said.

When I went back to the club, there were several girls who asked how it went. I told them about my diagnosis and treatment plan. I was only kind of surprised to learn that all of the girls who went to Dr. Bob had exactly the same problem as I did. That would seem to make sense seeing as we all wore the same goofy shoes and did the same job. As we discussed our mutual back problems, I started to get a little suspicious, though. It would seem to make sense that we would have some of the same physical problems, but it seemed odd that we would all have exactly the same issues. The only thing that differed were the treatment and payment plans. If we all had the same problem, wouldn't the treatment and payment plans be the same, too?

This is where I started to wonder about Dr. Bob. I wasn't ready to pull the plug just yet, so I did a little more asking around. I talked to one of the bouncers who was a patient of Dr. Bob's also and was not all that surprised to learn that he and I shared the same back problems. The exact same problem. I glanced down to check the guy's shoes. When I saw he was in sneakers, I began to suspect that Dr. Bob might be a liar. The bouncer then discussed with me his treatment schedule and payment plan. I was not shocked to learn that his payment plan was significantly lower than mine and the girls'. I wasn't sure I liked Dr. Bob anymore.

I decided at that point it might be a good idea to learn a little more about chiropractic care and their practitioners. I went to the library, the prehistoric google. It turned out that Dr. Bob was not, in fact, a doctor. Having debunked homeopathy during my ill-fated high school report on the subject, I was familiar with the idea of pseudoscience, but it had never occurred to me that chiropractic care also fell into that category. I didn't like Dr. Bob anymore. Even if he didn't try to grope me during an exam.

You're Going to Be a Star

Around the same time that I knew Dr. Bob, in the same topless bar I met a guy who said I was going to be a star. That you've never seen me walk the red carpet might give you just a little hint as to where this is going. As a stripper, I have on several unfortunate occasions met a pimp or two. They are usually easy to spot. They tend to look like the stereotypical pimp, with stupid outfits and even stupider high opinions of themselves. For the most part, they are pretty easy to avoid, but every once in a while, one slips through the cracks.

This particular pimp presented himself as a talent agent. I suppose he technically was. This guy's name was Rick. He told my friend and I that we should be doing magazines. The internet did the same thing to nudie magazines as it did to the libraries. Print resources for naked people and research information, it seems, have both become obsolete. But back in dinosaur times, my friend and I were terribly flattered to be told that we would be in magazines. So naturally, we jumped in his, not joking here, vintage Cadillac and drove with him down to the porn capital of the country, the San Fernando Valley in Southern California.

Rick was a talent agent for nude models. When you're under five foot eight, nude modelling is, or was, pretty much the only kind of modelling available to you. I knew when I stopped growing at age thirteen I was not likely to be strutting my stuff on the catwalks of Paris. Posing for Hustler seemed like the next best thing. It helped that Woody Harrelson had done a fabulous job of making Larry Flynt seem like a champion for the first amendment. While I mostly agree with that, the reality is that Larry is still kind of a jerk face when it comes to women's rights. Either way, I was going to be a Hustler honey, and that was pretty bitchin. Rick had all but promised us that we were going to not just do Hustler, but a whole host of other magazines as well. My friend and I were too excited to see the multiple bright red flags that Rick was waving in our faces.

Halfway down to LA, Rick was pulled over in his pimp mobile. He did not have a valid driver's license. The only reason we were allowed to continue on our journey south was because I was the only person in the car who did. The cop let him go with only a ticket on the condition that I would drive the rest of the way. Prior to this incident, Rick was lecturing my friend and me about responsibility. He was not thrilled that we enjoyed smoking marijuana and told us that it would make us lazy and that potheads never got their shit together. After getting pulled over, I was tempted to lecture him on the various definitions of irony, but I decided to let it go. I didn't want to squander my chance at stardom.

After reaching our destination, instead of accepting Rick's offer to stay at his house, we finally made a reasonable decision and got a hotel. Rick had described his house as an elegant, almost mansion, in an upper class suburban neighborhood. The only thing he described accurately was its size. The house was rather run down and there were already a number of soon-to-be stars staying there. One thing we noticed about our fellow models was that they appeared to be particularly subdued. We found out later that although Rick was not a fan of marijuana, he had no issues with cocaine or heroin. Or any other drug that might make someone numb and or more complacent. The flags Rick was throwing up were becoming more and more apparent, but we still had stars in our bloodshot eyes.

Eventually, we made it to the Hustler building to meet with the people who would make us pin-up stars. We could hardly contain our excitement, right up until the point when they swiftly ushered us out the door. It would seem that our talent agent/pimp had sold us as want-to-be porn stars. While he told us that we would only do print work, he was telling Larry's people that we were ready to do hard core porn movies. That was not quite what we had in mind and nothing even close to what we agreed to. We were now able to see the red flags that had totally engulfed us. Rick, like Dr. Bob, was not what he seemed.

While that should've been our clue to dump Rick and go home, we gave him one more chance. He had booked us for a relatively lucrative photo shoot for an internet site. It seemed pretty easy, and it would at a bare minimum give us something to take home from our trip. Once again, we were utterly blind to the warning signs that were right in front of our faces. First, to prepare for the shoot, they didn't want us to have much makeup. Although we were twenty-one, we both looked really young, and we looked practically childlike without eyeliner. Second, about halfway through the shoot, we were presented with a basket of dildos. When I say basket, I mean a large plastic laundry basket filled with rubber penises. That was when I was officially done with Rick. It took a basket of dildos to finally make me see that Rick was a fraud and a liar. I probably don't have to mention that Rick had not specified that this shoot would require penetration, something we made clear before getting into his car that we were not willing to do.

It took about a dozen phone calls before I found a rental car agency that would rent a car to someone under twenty-five. Feeling dejected and really stupid, we made our way back home. We were supposed to know better. Being in a business where we were the ones who were selling a fantasy, it was really hard to admit that we had been sold one. We got so caught up in what we wanted to believe that we were blinded to the reality that was right in front of us all along. We bought into the fallacy that this guy was selling.

Dr. Bob was selling the same sort of fallacy. He presented himself as something he wasn't. If I had bothered to check out Rick in the same way, we might have avoided the whole fiasco. The only real difference between the two men was that one said he was a doctor.

Pseudo-Doctor

Dr. Bob was not a medical doctor. Chiropractors do go through a lot of school, but a good portion of it is learning about theories and – big shocker here – marketing. In the realm of pseudoscience and alternative medicine, chiropractic is a little tricky. Most chiropractic practitioners today use a mix of mainstream medicine along with the not-so-mainstream ideas behind chiropractic theories. This helps to ensure they get covered by some medical insurance plans. There is little to no scientific evidence to suggest that chiropractic medicine has any benefit by itself, except in some cases relieving minor low back pain. Most of the treatments today include things like massage, heat, and ice therapy, which are proven to be effective in relieving pain. Spine manipulation alone, though, has not been shown to be effective at all, and in some cases can lead to injury and even death. I know, I'm kind of a buzzkill, but I may have just saved you a ton of cash.

On its surface, alternative, or natural, medicine seems like a no brainer. And it is, if you don't think about it. People will talk about ancient medicine being effective and sometimes better than mainstream medicine. The fact is that when ancient or alternative medicine is proven to work, it becomes mainstream medicine. Leeches are a great example of this. While super gross, these foul creatures have been used in medical treatments for thousands of years. When bloodletting was a thing, they were supposed to remove impure blood to cure disease. That isn't quite what they are used for today. If you have ever seen the show "Botched" where plastic surgeons fix bad plastic surgery, you will sometimes see them put leeches on nipples or noses to facilitate blood flow. As disgusting as that is, leeches are an ancient form of natural or alternative medicine that is now considered mainstream. Cracking your spine to improve your bowel functions or relieve headaches is not.

Of all the things that I talk about that aren't what they seem, alternative medicine gets me the most push back. I am apparently the Debbie Downer of alternative medicine. I'm really OK with that. I've been called much worse. The fact is that sometimes it can be hard to distinguish between pseudoscience and established science. I was surprised to learn that there is no actual accepted definition of the word *Natural*, which allows it to be used indiscriminately in advertising. There are in fact, a whole lot of things that are natural which will kill you. Hemlock, rhubarb leaves, and ricin are all natural, so is mercury, and arsenic, but you don't see those things being sold as healthy in Trader Joe's. The Botox I put in my face is derived from *natural* botulism, but I still require a medical doctor to administer it.

While I will fully admit that not all medical doctors are ethical or not motivated by money, mainstream medicine is far more reliable than the alternative or natural type. There are plenty of home remedies and treatments that are effective. Ginger for upset stomachs has been used for thousands of years, and I can say personally, it works. Epsom salts for muscle aches is another good one, ear candles however, are bullshit. Telling the difference can be tricky.

Pseudoscience is not exclusive to medicine. Astrology, intelligent design, numerology, are all fabulous examples of nonsense masquerading as science. The vast majority are designed to push an agenda as in the case of intelligent design, or to sell you something like a daily personalized horoscope. I worked as a phone operator before I started dancing, I basically answered the call-in lines for TV ads. One product I sold was a fat pill that was supposed to absorb the fat in your food to help you lose weight. If you watched the ad, you would likely be convinced that it was based on scientific fact. However, it was based on complete bullshit that sounded like scientific fact. The only scientifically proven effect of this product was diarrhea and nausea. So, really, it could help you lose weight, if only because you were either stuck on the toilet or too nauseated to eat. I was eventually fired from this job because I told a crying overweight teenager to discuss diet and exercise options with her doctor and not to waste her $300 on these stupid pills. I never once regretted the decision to tell that girl the truth. The fat pills I was pushing were a bogus and unethical attempt to capitalize on someone's problem.

There are some things not based on real science that can be super comforting and effective. I have found yoga to be extremely helpful in terms of alleviating anxiety and improving flexibility. I don't, however, believe that yoga has any effect on my chakra or aura like the yoga instructor I follow on YouTube would have me believe. I know that the deep breathing, balancing, and stretching has a real effect on my brain and body. The simple act of focusing on my breathing and movements is highly effective in stopping the anxiety hamster in my brain from running around my head telling me I should be worried about everything. Knowing that yoga has no effect on my non-existent aura doesn't stop me from benefitting at all from this ancient exercise. The pants are wicked comfortable too.

As a dancer I made a point to build strong personal boundaries when it came to customers. Still, there were many guys who I genuinely liked and that I trusted. Knowing who to trust in the strip club can be almost impossible. The same can be said of science or medical information. Finding a balance between who to trust and who to run screaming from is really hard and Dr. Bob was not the only guy who fooled me into trusting him. Because most dancers are independent contractors, medical insurance was not something most girls had. Dr. Bob was so appealing because he seemed to be offering medical services that dancers needed.

Rick was much the same in this respect. He was selling what we thought we needed, stardom. Pseudoscience is like the talent agent telling you what you want to hear. It depends on the listener not vetting the information they are being presented. It relies on your willingness to believe what you want to, while ignoring the red flags that are ultimately waving in your face. Like Rick, alternative medicine and other pseudoscience hides behind a smokescreen of crap that sounds really good, but really has no substance to it at all. It sells a simple answer to complicated problems.

Pseudoscience sometimes uses unproven science or skews information in a way that makes it sound legitimate. Like Bob and Rick, sellers of pseudoscience saw a desire or a problem and just happened to have an answer that we wanted to hear. Because we are inundated with information, learning how to distinguish what is real and what is just trying to get you to buy something is really important. A good rule of thumb is to look for various sources of the claims being made. Look for other sources showing the same information, to see if it aligns with the information you first saw. If multiple sources are saying the same thing, you should be able to figure out whether something is worth your time and money.

As someone who spent more than half my life selling a fantasy, I can say that the best way to get someone to buy something is to tell them exactly what they want to hear. Like, I can cure your back pain, or I will make you a star. Spotting the pimp pretending to be a talent agent, or the quack pretending to be a doctor, can be one of the most important tools you can learn in life. My suggestion would be to apply a little skepticism to any claims that seem too good to be true. Do some digging, and check out the claims being made, even if that person tells you they're a doctor or that they will make you a star. Don't wait for a basket of dildos to be the final clue that you put your faith in the wrong person.

Chapter 18

Call Me a Stripper

Being Yourself Brings Real Friends

"What made you want to be a stripper, oops, sorry. I mean Exotic Dancer?" The questions people ask me vary. Sometimes, it's wondering how I started, how my marriage works, or how I deal with the stigma and stereotype of stripping. The question isn't really the issue for me. It's that people will apologize for using the word *stripper*. As if somehow the word itself is an insult, or somehow offensive. When people apologize for using the word, it is almost always because they are genuinely concerned that I might have taken offense by it. One thing I want to make clear is that I don't. Depending on the person or the context of the conversation, I may correct them and say, "Stripper is fine. Dancing is kind of a lofty word for what I do."

In an ironic twist, I actually kind of consider using the word dancer to describe what I do as an insult to professional dancers. I didn't train for years with a coach. I've never carefully crafted my moves to be meticulously on time with the beat. I've never worked with or even considered using a choreographer. Because that would just be stupid. The entire point to my performance is to get naked, or to strip. So, the word stripper is acutely accurate. That is exactly what I do, or did, strip. To get offended by the word stripper is to say that I am somehow ashamed of what I did. If you haven't figured it out by now, I'm not.

When someone refers to me as an exotic dancer, it is to soothe their discomfort with the topic. While I appreciate that someone is going out of their way to not offend me, it's almost as offensive to assume that I may take offense to the word stripper in the first place. To use, in my opinion, the obvious misnomer *dancer*, is to conceal the true nature of the job. If I am comfortable with what I do, I don't need to hide or come up with a better sounding word or phrase than stripper. The word stripper has many negative connotations attached to it sometimes, and I understand by using a different term someone may be trying to separate the stigma from the job. That is a nice thing to do, but it would be nicer to not have those stigmas attached to the word stripper *at all*.

The fact is, and I'm probably repeating myself here, there is nothing wrong with stripping. The reason that I find the word dancer used in describing the profession as insulting to professional dancers, is not that stripping isn't a legitimate occupation, it's that dancing is not the main component. Stripping requires just as much effort and sometimes hardship as being a professional dancer, whether ballet, or working in a stage show, or even shaking your ass in a music video. It's all hard work. Stripping involves preparation, a specific wardrobe, a certain level of fitness, auditions, and in many other ways parallels mainstream dancing. The real difference is that you can be a terrible dancer and still be a successful stripper.

By terrible dancer I mean exactly that. I can't tell you how many strippers I've seen that would make Tony Basil break out in hives. Still, those same strippers will make hundreds of dollars off of one stage in minutes. Meanwhile, you have professional cheerleaders who go through a massive amount of training, travel, and who knows what, struggling to make even basic living expenses. To conflate the two and call the one who can simply get naked to make oodles of cash a dancer kind of sucks for the one who spends years perfecting complicated moves for peanuts. I'm not necessarily saying one is better than the other, just that it is unfair to say that the two professions are the same. Strippers make their money getting naked and grinding in laps. Professional dancers, on the other hand, actually dance.

And yet, with all that being said, a good majority of the time, when asked what my profession is, I will say "exotic dancer". In some contexts, I'll proudly profess my stripper-ness, and in others, will carefully choose my words in fear of the reaction I may get. While I do get annoyed with other people trying to sugar coat the profession, I do the exact same thing. I choose to be a hypocrite in

158

this way because of the stereotypes associated with the word, regardless of the fact that it is the more accurate depiction of my job. For twenty years I have tried to overcome the stigma and judgements that come with my job. I've written and published two books on the subject, and yet I am still reluctant to call myself what I really am. A stripper.

I thought I had overcome the fear of telling people that I was a stripper when my first book was published. In fact, that was the whole point in writing it. To come out as proud and unashamed of my job. To show the people who called me a whore, or a druggie, or even a bad mom, my acrylic tipped middle finger. I feel like I succeeded, to a point. I put out a counterpoint to the stereotypical stories that drive the negative stereotype. By documenting my story, I was hoping to embolden other dancers who liked their jobs and weren't damaged and broken like so many try to tell us we are. To be proud, too. To know that they had someone trying to defend them and their choices. Writing my story helped me to accept myself and my choices.

Recently, I was talking with someone, discussing working hard and achieving goals, and I mentioned that being a stripper helped me get to where I am. The person I was talking to, said, "Well, you did what you had to do."

To which I immediately replied, "No, I did what I wanted to do. I am not ashamed, nor do I regret being a stripper. I liked my work and I am proud of it. I wrote two books about it."

She appeared taken aback and then said, "Oh, well, good for you, I guess."

I hoped that by coming out I would finally be free of worrying about what other people think, and I think I am for the most part. Writing helped legitimize my job in some sense because it is counterintuitive to think that a stripper could also be a writer. By becoming an author, I have been able to show people in a very powerful way that I have accepted myself as a stripper, and that what other people think doesn't matter. Now, if I can only bring myself to call myself a stripper *all* the time…

Another Dirty Word

Once I got to a certain level of comfort being open about being a stripper, I thought I had exposed all that I had hidden. I had taken a bold and brazen step to tell the world what I am. Fuck you all, I am what I am, deal with it. I thought that I had stuck it to all the people who felt I should be ashamed of myself. I am an open book, literally. I have opened myself up and revealed all that I am supposed to keep hidden. I was surprised, actually, that while I still catch some crap for being a stripper, a good portion of people were more than happy to accept it and move on. Many asked questions that allowed me to clarify and dispel the misconceptions. All told, it was really a good thing, even if I pussyfoot around it once in a while. I didn't think that there was anything else about myself I had to hide, or anything that would bring the same kind of judgement. I couldn't have been more wrong.

I had been keeping another secret, one that would bring a much harsher backlash than stripping ever could have. It never occurred to me that anything could be as socially unacceptable as being a stripper. Deep down I knew, I just never admitted that I was deliberately concealing another part of myself from not just the world at large, but my family and friends, too. It was almost as if coming out a stripper was simply another way of hiding what I was afraid of saying. In relation, being an unabashed stripper was much easier than being an unabashed atheist.

For a very long time, I have been fairly open about my rejection of organized religion. Taken objectively, the ideas behind the Catholic faith that I was raised in are pretty ridiculous. I was never really embarrassed when attending a funeral or wedding in a Catholic church to be the heathen sitting in the pew, while everyone else got their cracker and wine. Despite being curious as to what they tasted like, the symbolism of eating flesh and drinking blood is pretty easy for me to dismiss as disturbingly goofy. Most people understood why I would reject that kind of ritual. I never caught any meaningful flak for calling out that bullshit. Most people, even Catholics, were sympathetic to my objections. *As long as you believe in something*, they were cool.

160

Belief in any higher power is enough for most people to be comfortable. The universe, karma, or whatever, as long as you believe in something, you're cool. I think a lot of people consider even just the concept of god to be subjective. It's personal. You are free to believe in whatever you want as long as you believe there is something greater than you. When you say you don't believe in any type of higher power, that is when you see the real contempt, and hostility.

"You're a stripper? Good for you, you're so brave, I wish I had that kind of confidence."

"Oh, you're an atheist? Your life has no meaning, how can you have any morals? Aren't you afraid of hell?" I discovered that the word atheist has as many if not more negative connotations as the word stripper. I found that as I was careful using the word stripper, I also had to be careful using the word atheist. Sometimes even more so. The definition of the word atheist is simply someone who doesn't believe in a god. That could mean anything from belief in no gods at all, or that one doesn't believe in one specific god, like Thor. In the interest of full disclosure, if he looks like the guy who plays Thor in the movies, I might be willing to believe. Put in those terms, almost everyone is an atheist, really, you only have to not believe in one god. Taken at face value, the actual meaning of the word is pretty benign, and yet it can invoke extreme offense in some people.

Freethinker is in my opinion the nicer word for atheist. Like the term *exotic dancer,* it gives a moment to explain the position without using the word that has such stigma attached to it. Although I think it can be just as accurate as atheist, it is a kinder, gentler way of putting it. Once you've made clear to the other person that you're not a serial killer with no moral guide, you may be able to get them to understand that atheist isn't the dirty evil word that it can seem to be. Sometimes, using the word atheist right out front, shuts down the conversation. It's like you just walked up to them and pissed on their leg. It can buy you a little time to explain the meaning of the word, before they turn and walk away in disgust.

Most people who have known me would say that overall, I am an honest and kind person. I try my best to help people where I can and to be a good person, even if I can be a little crude and brash sometimes. A sort of strange amnesia takes over when I say I don't believe in a god, or that I'm an atheist. All of a sudden, the same people who think I'm a good person will suddenly question my goodness. As if being an atheist negates the good things I do in my life. Like I've grown horns on my head and hooves have instantly replaced my feet. The hostility in some cases by the people who were so willing to accept me as a stripper is not only hurtful, but disturbing.

There are people in my life whom I had considered role models in ethics and morality who, once they found out that I didn't believe in God, said some horribly hurtful things. Sometimes even refusing to believe that I didn't believe, completely rejecting my view. I can understand the fear that someone might feel if they truly believe that their loved one is going to burn for eternity. That would certainly make them want to change my position. If you saw someone who was about to jump off a bridge, any decent human being would want to change their mind. You would go out of your way to stop them. What you wouldn't do would be to insult their intelligence, tell them they're wrong or stupid. And yet that is exactly the reaction I have gotten in some instances. The rejection I have faced when revealing my disbelief is unsettling and makes me question the very foundations of how I was raised. That some of my relationships are dependent on my belief in a deity shook me to the core.

Not all of the believers in my life have been this harsh. When I discussed it with my mom, she simply thought about it and adjusted her belief. She changed her position from 'well as long as you believe in something God will let you into heaven', to 'as long as you're a good person'. She told me that she found comfort in her beliefs, but also found it important to be accepting of mine. She confessed her own doubts about God and told me that she chose to believe. Her willingness to accept me made me able to find comfort with the priest in her last hours. I knew that it would be a comfort to her, and so it was a comfort for me, even if I didn't ascribe any supernatural powers to the prayers he offered.

Somewhere in between the rejection and acceptance of my atheism is the passive aggressive approach. There are those who will choose to interject a snide remark here and there to gauge my reaction. These comments feel like a provocation to argument. I usually try not to take the bait. When I first came out, I felt a need to argue my case against God, and sometimes I still do. But for the most part, I understand that it is a personal thing for people and challenging a belief system that has been the basis of one's life invokes a strong cognitive dissonance. Unless someone is using their belief or religion in order to be hurtful, I leave it alone.

Some people simply need that belief, and I see no reason to not let them have it. I have had many productive conversations with people who believe. These kinds of conversations are not to persuade but to gain an understanding. I have left these discussions with a better sense of the person I was talking to and found myself in a position to be more accepting of a position that I do not hold. In many cases, been left feeling closer to that person as well.

When someone tries to use religion as a weapon to judge, subjugate, or otherwise compromise my personal freedoms or the freedom of my child, well, now we have a problem. A big one. I simply refuse to allow another's belief system to dictate my life. A way to clarify that point is to give an example of making others bend to your will. It would be like someone saying, "I don't want to be a stripper", and my reply being, "You have to if you don't want to be punished."

Our country guarantees us certain freedoms, you are free to any religion you choose or to choose no religion at all. Just as you are free to be a stripper and free to not be. It is absolutely that simple. Forcing someone to be a stripper would be universally seen as an infringement on personal freedom. I view, as does our constitution, forcing religion on other people as the same infringement on personal freedom.

Secular Stripper

Revealing my atheism left me distant from some people I had been close to at one point. The relationships were not lost completely but changed. Whereas before, I felt like I had to pretend to believe, now that they knew, it was like they just now noticed the elephant in the room that had always been there for me. A subject to be avoided. A certain weirdness crept into the conversations and left

163

me much more closed off than I was before. A strange feeling of distance that seemed impossible to overcome. Around the people with whom I had previously found comfort, I no longer felt like I had a place. I chose to focus on my son and husband and looked to find peace with the newly strained relationships in my life.

Writing about my experiences helped me to let go, and to find acceptance with myself and newly expressed atheism. I decided to submit an article to a non-profit organization I was a member of. The Freedom From Religion Foundation had written a letter to my school district on behalf of my 5th grade son, who had been sent home with a flyer promising him a free bike if he attended a church event. FFRF is an organization dedicated to the separation of church and state. They work tirelessly to defend the part of the first amendment that guarantees freedom *of* religion as well as freedom *from* religion. They accepted my writing, and it was published in the following month's national newsletter.

FFRF's annual convention was scheduled to be in San Francisco shortly after that. I thought, fuck it, let's go see what it's all about. A weekend by the ocean with someone else to do the cooking and laundry sounded lovely. I had emailed the editor of the FFRF publication a few times, and had friended him on social media, so I figured I would know someone. Although, I do regret not snooping his profile a little because had I known he was like seven feet tall, I would've worn heels.

I walked into the first speaker presentation with some pamphlets I had picked up with not much of a clue who the speaker was. A man named Salman Rushdie was talking. Thirty seconds into his talk, I regretted not knowing who he was. First, he is a dynamic speaker, and second, he wrote a controversial book that put his life in danger. By the time he was finished speaking, I was left with the knowledge that I had a lot to learn and was excited to start, and this was just the first night.

When I found the editor I knew, he introduced me to someone who, in turn, introduced me to the president of my local chapter, a lovely lady named Judy Saint. Judy, as it would happen, turned out to be more of a muse than a saint. She invited me to sit with her and her wife during the first of the day's presentations. While we waited for it to start, I told her that I was an exotic dancer,

164

watching carefully for the judgmental reaction that never came. When I told her about some of the rejection I had faced for both being a stripper and an atheist, she turned to me, looked me square in the eye, and said, "You're home." Astonished, I had to fight back tears because, until then, I hadn't quite realized how isolated coming out as an atheist had made me feel. That isolation made me feel like I was falling. The atheist community provided me a soft place to land.

Being a stripper in some sense was also isolating. The camaraderie I felt in the presence of other strippers helped, but most of the time I didn't have much else in common with them. This felt much different. Like a warm hug from a thousand people. Every meal, I sat at a different table with new people and learned a little more. The acceptance and understanding from the people I met was truly mind blowing. Because atheists usually come from a place of logic, reason, and curiosity, almost no one even flinched when I told them my past profession. There was no inherent judgment about what I did, plenty of questions, but none that felt intended to be cruel. One lady asked me if I had ever had a drug problem, which is a common stereotype about strippers, but was willing to learn and listen to me when I explained that I hadn't.

Accepting and taking ownership of who I am as a stripper led me to write my first book. Accepting my atheism led me to find others who thought the same. Once I learned to accept who I was and to stop apologizing for it, I found that there were many people who also accepted me for who I was. I was so afraid of being judged for being different, and so intent on conforming and pretending to be what I wasn't, that I never stopped to think that there were people who would accept me for who I am. I didn't need all that pretending. I am what I am. I'm not sorry for it. And that is perfectly awesome. On the last day, I spoke with the editor, telling him how many wonderful people I had met. He informed me that I had become known as the Secular Stripper. *Secular Stripper*, I thought. I can live with that.

Since then, I have done so much reading and learning, and found a welcoming community that pales in comparison to any church I ever went to. Of course, there are differing opinions, and viewpoints, but the very fact that the atheist and skeptical community deals with science and facts means that every disagreement is an opportunity to learn. If there is one thing that the atheists have in common, it is a willingness to learn, a hunger for knowledge. Real knowledge and accepting the things that we don't know. Instead of making up things to explain what we don't know about our world, each unknown is viewed as a chance to find the answer. If there is anything at all we can be sure of, it is that there is an endless opportunity to learn new things about the world and the creatures living in it.

Each one of us is unique in our own way. We are all different, and sometimes those differences can make us feel alone. It takes a lot of courage to embrace what makes us different. Whether it be ideologically, physically, or if you happen to get naked for a living, accepting yourself for who you are can be daunting. The need to blend in and not stand out is tempting when you know you are risking disapproval from the very people you care about. What I found, is when I was finally able to accept myself, there was a whole community of people ready to accept me for who I was, too.

If there is one thing you take away from this book, I hope it is that you know that however you are different, you are not alone. There is someone out there who understands. There are people out there, probably many, who have gone through what you have. Or have faced the same things you have and are more than happy to accept you for who you are. In turn, you might be the very person someone else is looking for. Someone who may have felt abandoned, themselves, for being different. Stripper, atheist … words are just words. While they have their definitions, they don't totally define us as people. We have to accept the fact that we have the power to define ourselves, and ultimately the only opinion that matters is our own.

Chapter 19

More Than a Pair of Boobs

You Might Be a Humanist

Late at night, close to closing, I walk around topless. Strolling down the aisle in a grocery store half naked would not be okay, but in the strip club this is totally acceptable. Another perk of the job. In most situations I tend to think of myself as a minimalist, especially in terms of fashion choices. In the strip club I've always opted for the less is more approach. When I first starting stripping, a lot of girls wore elaborate costumes and made a big show of it. I tried, but soon found that pulling off a pair of bell bottoms while trying to look graceful was simply not going to work for me. So, I went for simple bikinis and things like that. Easy to get in and out of. At the end of the night when I was ready to leave the club, I would have everything packed up, and would then finish out the night in just a G-string.

Most of the time when guys come to the club an hour before it closes, they don't want to waste any time, and are ready for lap dances. Earlier, it is a good idea to let them get settled and get a drink, you don't want to rush. Guys will usually turn down the first girl who walks up, especially if the guy just sat down. Later, it's different. You can walk right up and take them back to the VIP room. If I'm already topless, I'm ahead of the game. While going around without a top started as a convenience, it ended up being an interesting social experiment.

In a regular social setting, guys will usually go out of their way to make sure they are not looking at your chest. In the strip club it's not like that, until you approach them topless. I started to notice that when I had a top on, guys would be desperately looking at my boobs. Late at night without a top, most guys would do the opposite. I mean, I have my top off. You would think they would be encouraged to look, but they don't. The majority of the time, when I'm approaching a strip club customer topless, they go out of their way to look me in the eye. I found this highly amusing and started to challenge them. I would ask them why they weren't looking at my boobs. Put on the spot, most guys would kind of act embarrassed and say things like, "I was trying to be polite". Funny, that they would be polite now, when I'm literally asking them to look.

When a customer remembers my name, I usually say something like, "Thanks, most people just remember my boobs." In the strip club, I expect to be treated like an object. I'm not offended by it. That is what I chose to do. I didn't have any illusions that I wouldn't be treated like a sex object, that is very much a part of the job. When guys don't treat me that way, I am always pleasantly surprised. What is it about being almost naked that seems to inspire most guys to try to be more considerate of my feelings? In other social settings, guys still treat me like an object, even when I'm dressed in my mom clothes with hardly any make up. I've been cat-called walking with my son. There was even a case where some guy was shadowing me in the grocery store. Normally, I let my kid go off on his own, but I needed him to stay close this time to discourage this guy from approaching me. Which he did anyway, although, credit is due my son who gave him the stink eye over my shoulder, until the guy finally walked away.

There seems to be something about being topless in the strip club that reminds guys that I am more than a pair of boobs. It's like the dog who is trained to be patient while balancing a treat on their nose. Putting boobs in a guy's face seems to make them more aware of their behavior. It's like my exposed breasts remind them that I am a human being. Which is even funnier when you realize that my boobs are mostly silicone and saline, and probably the least human thing about me.

We're All Human

When on the phone with an uncooperative customer service representative, or dealing with an exceptionally difficult DMV employee, it can be hard to remember that we are all human. We have far more in common with each other than not. It seems so easy to look at other people with disdain and hostility when they don't seem to be behaving in a way that suits us at that moment. We are so quick to judge someone an asshole without really having any real idea of who that person is, or what they may have gone through. Driving in traffic is like that. We see the cars in our way and forget that a human being is behind the wheel. Surrounded by two thousand pounds of metal, the person in the car effectively ceases to exist.

When I chose to become a stripper, I actively accepted that I would be treated as less than human, but in the real world it seems like it happens much more often. In almost every situation it can feel like the people we are dealing with forget that we are all part of the same species. We tend to categorize each other, we put each other in groups, assign numbers, or otherwise try to distance ourselves from our collective humanity. The dehumanizing we do to each other is almost systemic.

When we get wrapped up in our own bullshit it can be easy to forget that other people are likely dealing with their own bullshit as well. It is far easier to view them as so different than ourselves that they may no longer appear human to us. This is especially true in online social media. When we aren't dealing with people face to face, or boobs to face as in my case, people aren't people anymore. They are a digital approximation of a human. Looking at a carefully chosen profile pic, which in some cases isn't even themselves, identifying them as a person with feelings and emotions is almost impossible. Seeing people as human has become even more difficult. People now hide behind online personas that may or may not reflect who they really are. Disassociating the person from the profile allows some truly hateful interactions. Protected by a false image, people online are free to spew insults and hate without seeing the real effect their words may have on the human being they have chosen to target. They are able to gain a small superficial amount of gratification by expressing things they would not do in person. They can spread rumors and false information without the benefit of seeing the real consequences of their actions or words.

It may seem that when we create an online image, we are free to be who we want, but that is an illusion. More often than not, hiding behind a keyboard brings out the worst in us. It allows us to be what we really aren't. Recently, a friend and I were talking about a stripper we had worked with back in the day. We haven't seen her in person in at least fifteen years, yet online she appears to not have aged in the slightest. Not a wrinkle, even well into her forties. As an avid Botox connoisseur, I can tell you that it does wonders, but not to that extent. Since we are both slightly younger, we were perplexed and definitely jealous. This lady has thousands of friends and followers online. Green with envy, I decided to dig a little deeper into her Facebook page.

To give just a little context, my computer class in high school had a dozen computer monitors. The biggest challenge was trying to get the only one that was in color. My earliest writing was done on a machine we called a "word processor". If you don't know what that is, look it up. I know, I'm like two steps away from yelling at the damn kids to get off my lawn. I've mostly caught up but am still relatively ignorant when it comes to a lot of computer programs and software. When I went to my former colleague's page, I went through her profile pics and finally recognized that every picture used a filter. I never used this feature, personally, because I could never figure out how to not make myself look like I was obviously using a filter, an art my old acquaintance has apparently mastered. I thought I would check out pictures of her that she hadn't taken herself and was not that surprised to see that she was always hiding behind a hat, or sunglasses, or found some other way to not show her face unfiltered. I stopped being jealous at that point.

What made me feel jealous was not real. This lady probably looked just as old as me. Which is not that bad, I feel the need to tell you. In fact, I started to feel bad for her. Don't get me wrong, even older, she was and probably is one of the most beautiful people I've ever seen. I mean, perfect in almost every way. I'd love to tell you that she is a bitch, but the truth is I've never known her in any meaningful way. Other than just superficial interactions, I really don't know her at all. What I do know is that she does not post any picture of herself without some sort of alteration. That would lead me to believe that she is not happy with her looks as she ages. Something I totally understand. When you've spent twenty years making money off your looks, every wrinkle on your face, or dimple on your ass, can be devastating. I've struggled with it myself, before coming to the realization that the only alternative to aging is death. Put that way, wrinkles and cellulite are preferable to being dead.

Altering your appearance in a photograph is easy. Accepting yourself the way you are is much harder, but well worth it in the long run. I'm not all the way there, as I still curse my grey hairs, but I'm working on it.

The bigger issue is that social media provides us with more chance to lie. Not only to other people, but to ourselves. When you are purposely hiding your true self from the world using a filter or some other new-fangled invention, you're also hiding from yourself. Is it possible to really accept yourself the way you are if you are constantly obscuring your faults? Who you are is probably not perfect. The good news is, neither is anyone else. The internet allows us to disconnect from the humanity of other people, but it also allows us to disconnect from our own humanity as well. It doesn't necessarily give us a chance to present to the world our real selves and feelings, so much as it gives us a chance to present a fake self. The version of yourself you choose to put online may in reality not only not be who you really are, but can make you act in ways that aren't true to yourself, either. I for one, have found myself being mean or judgmental online in a way that I would never do in person. I might see a post online and think, "What kind of jackass would post that?" only to realize that jackass was me.

When you are able to ignore the humanity in other humans, empathy becomes difficult. Seeing things from someone else's point of view is almost impossible. We may be able to feel popular online and gain a small amount of validation from likes and followers, but at what cost? Real human relationships and interactions become few and far between. Morals and ethics become blurry, whatever your ideology. Given the superficial world we have online, how do we reconnect with humanity?

Humanism

Ferris Bueller said, "Isms in my opinion are not good. A person should not believe in an ism, he should believe in himself." I agree with Ferris. "Isms" can be misinterpreted, taken to an extreme and lead to things that are not good. Of course, like just about anything, there are exceptions. When I started writing about

171

secular issues, I was concerned that I might be seen as having extreme views, maybe even considered militant. When someone asked me if atheists were radical, I explained that secular people, atheists, agnostics, and skeptics are some of the least radical people I have met. Made up of scientists, doctors, constitutional lawyers, and I mean this in the nicest of ways, a bunch of well-read nerds. At a gathering of atheists, what you won't see is a large angry mob yelling about the bible. What you are far more likely to see is people discussing books, scientific theories, and to my personal dismay, Star Trek.

That is not to say that there are no angry atheists. There are. I met a woman who had been part of a cult and subjected to a long and intense exorcism. She was pretty angry, but with good reason. The same goes for many others who were harmed by religion in one way or another. I listened to an Indian man who had witnessed his friends hacked to death by a machete. He was not so much angry, but scared. Their anger and hurt, though, seemed to be tempered by the sense of community they found in fellow atheists after they left their faiths. Even those types of people I wouldn't consider radical, if only because they were seeking to heal from their experiences. One of the things that endeared me to the other atheists I met was the love and acceptance of those who had been injured in some way by things they had been exposed to. Raised as a Catholic, to believe that people who doubted or didn't believe in God were incapable of love and inherently bad people, the reality couldn't be further from that. Without belief in an afterlife, or a judgmental deity, atheists don't have any real reason to make you not believe in God. There is really no reason to be extreme or militant. The only real beef with theism is when it interferes with a person's individual freedom. When it causes real harm. Although, of course, as with any group, there are those who feel the need to try to change people's minds and aren't always nice about it.

Atheists are, for the most part, also humanists. They base their beliefs and opinions on rational thought, empirical evidence, a healthy sense of skepticism, and a basic willingness to change their minds in the face of new information. All of those things are inconsistent with what we might consider radical or extreme. Ferris was right in that respect, that any view or "ism" taken to extreme is bad. Belief in yourself is a far better bet. Humanism is pretty much the idea that you believe in yourself and other people. Humanism

172

also provides a counterpoint to the idea that atheists have no moral code, no belief system on which to base their ethics.

Humanism, while being an ism, is the idea that you not only believe in yourself, but that you believe in the good in other humans, as well. It is an ideology for the secular, one that is based on critical thinking and empathy toward other people. It emphasizes the potential for good that humans have, focusing on the altruistic aspects of our species. That is not meant to imply that the world does not include a bunch of assholes mixed in with the altruistic people, it's just that humanists try to focus on the goodness in human nature itself. The basic concept of Humanism is to treat people with respect, kindness, and empathy. In other words, don't be an asshole. Not for fear of punishment or judgement, nor to get into heaven. In fact, you could even look at the idea of Humanism from the most selfish point of view possible, that doing nice things for other people simply makes you feel good. Most people like to see good things happen to other people. That's why when you see some sappy coffee commercial, or the fluff piece at the end of the news, you are left with the warm and fuzzies. Humanism, even in its most extreme form, is still pretty chill.

What I have found, diving into the atheist community, is a lot of open minds. The reactive pearl clutching that I was used to receiving when telling people about my work as an adult entertainer doesn't happen nearly as much. What I get mostly from atheists and the like is curiosity. Not that they all approve, just that they take some time to think about what they think about my job. Some disapproval still happens, but I am more willing to accept it if they have taken a moment to think, and not just recoil in revulsion. There is definitely something revolting about a boner in sweatpants, and I can dig it if someone is not totally on board with that. What I appreciate is the time taken to consider their thoughts before judgement.

While we are still confronted with unavoidable assholes, Humanism can make us stop and think about why that person is an asshole to begin with. The butthole at the DMV counter might be really tired of people simply assuming that they are a butthole. Maybe before you got up there, they had already dealt with fifteen or twenty people who had treated them like crap because they were annoyed, they had to go to the DMV in the first place. Speaking just for myself, after waiting in line or sitting in a plastic chair for an hour, by the time it's my turn, I may be itching for a confrontation.

How often do we take the time to consider other people's experiences and problems? I, for one, don't nearly as much as I should. Humanism offers that little nudge to think before we make judgments. A split second to wonder if there is a reason someone is acting rudely. Shortly after my mom died, I yelled at someone in the store for giving me what was a very benign and appropriate compliment. I'm sure that guy thought I was a bitch. Would he have thought that had he known that my mom had died only the night before? Not that it excuses my behavior – it doesn't – but it does offer a reason for it. I think he might have forgiven my rudeness if I had stopped to say that. What I did instead probably made him think twice about ever saying something nice to a stranger again. Not a good look.

By stripping as long as I have, I learned a very unexpected lesson about humanity. While I have written a lot about gross customers, or guys who are just assholes, really, most guys aren't like that. It's just that the nice ones aren't as interesting to write about. The vast majority of men who come into the strip club, though not the blackout drunk ones in a bachelor party, are simply looking for human connection. There are a lot of guys who just want a hug, or someone to listen to them. A good portion of guys aren't looking for sex, although there is an obvious sexual component, but just real human interaction. I have always kept very strict boundaries when it comes to men in the strip club, but I can't help the real feelings of empathy I may have toward some of the men I have dealt with.

Pure speculation here, but I think the reason men may react slightly differently when I approach them topless is that by being uncovered, they aren't faced with the boundary that clothing presents. I think that clothing provides a buffer from what we are underneath. Human. Ultimately, when we are faced with the bare essentials about what makes us people, it makes it easier to see things from someone else's perspective. After all, we're all naked underneath. Maybe clothes are just photo filters for our humanity. It seems that by being naked I am able to show people that I am more than a pair of boobs.

174

Chapter 20

Holidays for Heathens

Celebrate Everything – You're Alive!

There is anticipation mixed with just a little anxious energy in the air. The twinkling lights are hung, the sparkling garlands are strewn about the room, and the freshly cut tree is heavy with ornaments and even more lights. Snowmen and reindeer with red noses are dancing on the walls with angels. Brightly wrapped boxes, while empty, foreshadow the gifts that will be given when the special day finally arrives. The air outside is chilly, and inside, well, inside is chilly too, because it's always chilly in here. The spirit of giving is so much more pronounced this time of year. The hope is that all will come together just right to create the perfect celebration. Lists are made, who's naughty, who's nice, and who absolutely has to have a new Xbox. There is music in the air only heard once a year. Red hats with fuzzy white balls on them have come temporarily back in fashion. I know that all through this month, I will have the pleasure of seeing several jolly large bearded men in red suits. Possibly, just maybe, a light skinned man with brown hair and goatee, dressed in robes and sandals, will make his appearance and once again save my night. Last time Jesus was here, he spread a lot of joy even if he, very innocently I'm sure, forgot to wear underwear under his robes.

It's Christmas time in the strip club. The people who assert that Christ has been taken out of Christmas obviously haven't been to a strip club in a while, because that's precisely when he shows up. And true to the bible, he is kind and very generous. While I understand that in his time, underwear had probably not been invented yet, I do wish he would wear them anyway. His robes are quite thin and pretending to not notice the raging boner he is sporting becomes challenging at times, to say the least. Jesus has returned for his birthday party, and I am grateful he didn't show up in his birthday suit. He is very kind and generous, indeed.

Contrary to the Christmas bedtime stories, Santa prefers those on the naughty list. Just like the Santas at the mall, he likes girls to sit on his lap and tell him what they want for Christmas. Usually, though, he only offers one gift, and it's not a new teddy bear. When it comes to strip club Santa, cash is preferred to his candy cane, always. Customers who need a break from shopping or the stress of the impending holiday tend to be very giving that time of year. Because most guys take out cash for presents to prevent their significant others from seeing what they are buying, taking a little off the top for some stress relief is pretty common. Christmas provides a convenient way to conceal a little extra money spent on extracurricular activities. Strippers love Christmas.

Despite the festive costumes, religion is conspicuously absent from the holiday celebrations at the strip club, though it is still enjoyable and full of meaning. Presents, decorations, candy and all the other trappings still exist, yet there is no mention of Jesus, Mary, or the three wise men – with the exception of the guy who comes in dressed as the son of God. Despite the lack of religious meaning, the holiday still has the same magical feeling, even in this godless environment. The same expectations and giving spirit exist. Everyone says, "Merry Christmas." In the strip club there is no war on Christmas, quite the opposite, in fact. Christmas is alive and kicking with no signs of going away. How is it that the heathens in the strip club can celebrate a religious holiday with the same, if not more, passion than the Christians who claim it's being mercilessly attacked year after year? In my opinion, taking the Christ out of Christmas is what put the merry back in it.

Christ-less Christmas

Just as for many kids, Christmas was a magical time for me. I loved the songs, decorations, the presents, and the lights. Christmas lights have always been one of my favorite things about the season. When it is cold and dark outside, the lights bring a certain warmth to the night. Maybe they can be gaudy and slightly corny, but I love them, anyway. One thing that super sucked about Christmas, however, was having to go to church. All the stories about Santa Claus coming through just in time on the cartoon Christmas specials were crapped on by the actual story of Christmas. The son of God being born to a virgin, only to be tortured and executed because the humans that God created were so fucked up that he had to sacrifice his only son, sort of put a damper on the joy that Christmas brought. First, I had to learn what being a virgin meant, which was a little weird for a kid to learn. Then there was the whole crucifixion thing. Scary stuff for a little Catholic kid, or any kid for that matter. On Christmas, I always felt the need to say happy birthday to Jesus, and always added, "Sorry I am so bad that you had to die". But, then, I got presents and forgot about it.

While my old auntie's green gelatin mold, which was somehow both revolting and beautiful, was not my favorite thing about Christmas, it still holds a special place in my memories. As a kid, there was almost nothing quite as magical as Christmas. After the turkey bloat was gone, the anticipation for Christmas began, and it was awesome. I would slowly turn the pages of the Toys R Us catalog and meticulously circle the things I wanted Santa to bring me. I would start my homemade gifts and cards to proudly hand out to my family and friends. Each one unique and designed to show each recipient how much I appreciated them. I was almost as excited to see the look on their faces as they opened the artistic masterpieces that I had created, with construction paper, way too much glitter, and Elmer's glue, as I was to open my own gifts. The Christmas specials would start to play on TV, and to miss any of them, even GI Joe, bleh, would be devastating. The whole street lit up with lights, and the scent of the Christmas tree brought it all together. Then, like a pulsating pimple that shows up on prom night, Jesus would come and remind me that it was all about him.

Early in my childhood, my family didn't really go to church regularly, but we went on or around Christmastime and Easter. Nothing took the fun and wonder out of Christmas like walking into an old dark and spooky building, decorated with execution symbols and creepy imagery. Forced to hug weird old ladies, with perpetual looks of scorn and judgement on their faces, was one of the most challenging parts of this ritual. Watching people make the somber stroll up the aisle to get their blood and flesh always seemed kind of weird. In my head, I would think, "Don't eat that, it's gross!", but

177

the promise of presents for being good helped me from voicing this out loud. Jesus very nearly ruined Christmas every year.

As I got older, Christ became less and less a part of Christmas, yet the fun and joy was still there. I knew pretty early on that I didn't believe in the bible or Jesus. Once I started to think about the actual stories, none of it made any sense. I continued to pretend to believe in the same way I pretended to like the funky green Jell-O mold, but once I applied logic and reason to the religion I was raised in, I felt like I had no choice but to reject it as bullshit. I still loved Christmas, though, and all the holidays. Even Easter, whose story is one of the most fucked up things I can imagine celebrating. While the torture, and murder, in order to provide salvation to the people whom God designed as sinners in the first place, made for a disgustingly morbid tale to tell a kid, at least at Easter there were chocolate bunnies, jellybeans, and yet another weird Jell-O mold to make up for it.

Although I didn't identify as an atheist just yet, I knew that these were messed up reasons for holidays. I wondered if I should be celebrating them as a non-believer. Did I even have a right at all to participate in them? I read and learned, and soon discovered that most of the holidays I loved didn't really have their origins in Christianity to begin with. Wait, what? I was shocked and pleased to discover that most of the traditions that went along with the celebrations of virgin births and resurrections were actually Pagan in origin. In fact, Jesus wasn't born on December 25th. Christmas was deliberately moved to that date to coincide with the Pagan winter solstice. Easter is never on the same day because it was meant to align with the spring equinox. Christ was never in Christmas as we know it, to begin with. The goateed guy usurped this holiday for himself. I was not the interloper I thought I was in celebrating the holidays I had grown up with; Jesus was.

This realization begged the question, what am I celebrating? Without religious meaning, do holidays matter? Do they have a point, at all? The answer I came up with was hell yes, they have a point, and it has nothing at all to do with virgins, death, resurrection, or salvation.

Fuck It, Let's Celebrate

Atheists are often asked why they celebrate Christmas if they don't believe in a god. The best response to this I've seen came in meme form, that said, "Why do you celebrate Valentine's day if nobody likes you?" Or they may say things like, "Why would you say, 'Merry Christmas' if you don't believe the story of Christ?" Well, because it's tradition, it's cultural, and because it's just a nice thing to say. Just because I say "bless you" when someone sneezes doesn't mean I believe that their brains are leaking out of their heads and they need to be blessed by a god. I don't have to believe in a god to be polite. I love Christmas, and all the things that go with it. I'm perfectly OK leaving religion out of it.

The meaning behind the holidays we celebrate often have stupid, weird, and fucked up origins. Take Thanksgiving for example. It's great that we sat down and feasted with the native Americans before we gave them smallpox and drove them off their land. While I know the history, Thanksgiving is the one time of year when my whole family gets together to eat too much and to watch someone get really drunk and say something awful. Fun times. Cinco de Mayo is the celebration of a battle Mexico won, in the war they ultimately lost. Like St. Patrick's Day, now it's just an excuse to eat ethnically inspired food and drink too much. When you are drinking beer laced with green food coloring, are you really celebrating St. Patrick driving the snakes out of Ireland, or just making colorful barf? I would have to go with the latter. Halloween has odd meanings as well, but I love the scary movies, haunted houses, candy, and costumes; although, I get to dress in slutty costumes all year round, so that's not so special for me. There are many holidays whose origins and meanings have been lost, forgotten or are just plain disturbing. That's not necessarily a bad thing, because many of the reasons behind them are not things we would really want to celebrate.

Then you have holidays like New Year's Eve. That's a great reason to celebrate and get drunk, of course. A quick disclaimer: While I used to use these occasions to tie one on, as I've grown older, I have a greater appreciation for not ruining a whole day being hungover. These are times to reflect on the year past and look forward to the year ahead. Birthdays and weddings? Now, those are full of good and legitimate reasons to party. The Fourth of July is another great one, although I'm not a huge fan of fireworks. The point I am trying to make is: This life can super suck sometimes, and holidays, for whatever reason, make things a little more special. They give us a break from the same old thing. They give us a chance for reflection and appreciation of the things we have.

The meaning that we give to holidays, and really our own lives, are very much what we make them to be. For me as a kid, the holidays held a lot of meaning, but not what they told me it was. I wasn't celebrating the birth of Christ, I was celebrating family, friends, and even the hopelessly strange Jell-O mold. I was never a fan of school, didn't have a lot of friends, spent a lot of time with babysitters, and sometimes, even as a kid, life was kind of a bummer. Holidays were a bright spot when things sucked. A reminder that life is good and that I had many things to appreciate. Christmas, in particular, meant that for me. When it was cold and shitty outside, and I couldn't go swimming or do all the things I really liked, Christmas gave me something to look forward to. I got to see relatives I didn't see that often. I also got to experience the joy of giving to other people. Of course, I loved new toys, but even when I didn't get what I specifically asked for (I still have a slight pang of longing for the Teddy Ruxpin I never received), the joy and happiness were still there.

Many people hold the misconception that being an atheist or not ascribing to religion means that you are unable to find meaning in the holidays, or life itself. Frankly, that is one of the most insulting falsehoods about atheism. It implies that atheists have no reason to live, or that they live without meaning, while, ironically, the same people will wonder when some supernatural force will make their own life's meaning or purpose clear to them. I have some news for those people: The purpose and meaning in your life, and everyone else's, is exactly what you want it to be. Waiting for someone or something to show you your purpose is to waste the only time you know you have. It is up to you to decide what your purpose is. That can seem daunting, but it doesn't have to be. When you discover and accept that you are in control, it can be liberating.

Putting meaning and purpose in your life is in your control. You don't need to wait for some clandestine deity to show you your supposed path in life. Your path is whatever you want it to be, even if you make a wrong turn or two. Recognizing that there is no predetermined fate or destiny in your life allows you the freedom to decide for yourself, without having to wonder when someone will tell you what it is. Holidays and celebrations highlight the meaning and purpose we have in our lives already. They give us a chance to reaffirm what is already good in our lives, although for some, the holidays can do the opposite.

Sometimes holidays bring back awful memories, causing people to dread them instead of looking forward to them. Abuse, deaths, or just plain loneliness can make what should be a time of joy seem like a huge bummer. The birthday and Christmas I spent in boarding school were fucking awful. Seriously, they could not have sucked any more, but I choose to not let those times influence my future birthdays or Christmases. Why choose to hate those days just because one or two of them were so horrible? Every year is a new opportunity to make new happy memories. Deciding that Christmas or my birthday is going to be awful simply because one or more of them did is making the conscious decision to have another bad one. Frankly, that just makes it miserable for everyone else. I'm not sure I ever met anyone who hasn't had a shitty holiday at one point in time. One of the reasons I choose to host Christmas dinner is to help override the shitty holidays that people have had. My goal is to remind my friends and family that the past is in the past, and there aren't any days that need to be predetermined to suck.

Mother's Days, even though my husband and son always spoil me, have been a little rough without my mom. Mother's Day for me was always a time to celebrate my mom, make her favorite cake, lemon with white frosting, and let her know how much she meant to me. I can't do that in the same way, anymore. Her birthday is the same for me. She loved to be spoiled. Being unable to do that leaves me feeling a little empty. Finding a way to get through those days has been challenging, but I am starting to figure it out.

Chapter 21

Natural Born Skeptic

Raising a Freethinker

With so much candy stuffed between my legs, I found walking to be very difficult. My refusal to wear pants made this endeavor tricky. I was terrified that if I wore anything other than skirts or dresses I would be mistaken for a boy. I had a boy's name, but if I wore a dress, they had to know I was a girl. I believe one of the reasons I chose to be a stripper was this goofy feeling that I looked like a boy. I felt I had to prove I was not a boy by showing my genitals. "See? Look, I'm a girl!"

There were certain downsides to wearing only dresses, however. Stealing candy was one of them. My partner in this nefarious crime was a boy who lived a few houses down the street, and I swear it was his idea. We knew it was wrong, but we wanted candy, and at six years old we had limited financial resources. We both knew that if we were caught, we would be in big trouble, a fact that was making my fashion choice seem not just inconvenient, but dangerous. My friend could easily hide his loot in his pants. With no pockets, my underwear was the only hiding spot that my dress offered, and that just seemed gross. Although later in life, I would find that the side straps of my G-string would offer a convenient place to hold dollar bills. My solution with the candy, though, was to pin it between my thighs, but because it made me walk funny, doing so threatened to reveal our crime. Despite my impairment, we made it home without anyone noticing my odd gait. We were caught an hour later hiding in his backyard with crippling stomach aches surrounded by wrappers.

I was marched back to the store and made to confess and apologize to the store manager while my older brother paid for what we had stolen. Before committing the candy heist, my friend and I had discussed the consequences if we got caught. We knew we would be punished, maybe by grounding or loss of TV privileges. Those things were considered very serious. We also discussed the fact that we knew God was watching. He wouldn't be pleased, but he also wouldn't take away our cartoons. Quite the opposite, in fact. With God, we only had to ask for forgiveness. All we would have to do is pray for forgiveness and *poof*! we would be right with God. We could eat our stolen candy and still get into heaven. Getting caught by a human, well, that would suck big time, and it did.

Even with the knowledge that God would forgive me, I still felt guilty. Sure, getting caught, having to apologize, endure a long lecture from my brother, and losing a Saturday morning of cartoons was awful, but I still felt bad. I had taken my consequences and asked God and everyone else to be forgiven, and I was, but that shitty feeling lingered. Why would that be? I was raised with the idea that God was always watching but would forgive just about anything if you asked. Once forgiven, logic would dictate that the feelings of guilt would go away. What was there to feel guilty about? The candy was paid for and God forgave us. So, what the hell?

Around this time for me, I had started to doubt my belief in God. There were many things that just didn't seem consistent and caused me to question. For instance, I prayed every night for the starving children in Africa, who would apparently starve even more if I didn't eat my vegetables, but they were still starving. I prayed for world peace, but I still saw a lot of very unpeaceful things on the nightly news. And yet, when I prayed for a new dress, I got one. Those things seemed kind of messed up. Why the new dress but not feed the starving kids? The answer the adults gave was that God worked in mysterious ways. OK, but he seems like kind of an asshole. I then wondered if maybe I shouldn't have prayed for a new dress. Maybe God could only grant a certain number of prayers and started with the easy ones. If that was the case, then I shouldn't be praying for myself, as it was obvious to me that starving kids were more important than my new dress. One thing I knew for sure was that God was supposed to teach people to be good, yet he would forgive so quickly, without consequences. Even murder.

184

This stuff was really confusing, but eventually I came to the conclusion that God's forgiveness didn't change anything. Neither did losing a morning of TV, for that matter. What made me decide that stealing was wrong was the feeling of guilt that persisted, along with the fact that I had disappointed my family. It took a while to fully recognize it, but as I grew older, I understood that my sense of morality, empathy, and compassion didn't come from any god. I did think for a long time that going to church was what helped me understand how to decide what was right or wrong. I now know that wasn't true at all. What helped me understand right from wrong was not only how I felt when I did something wrong, but how it made other people feel, also. In fact, I came to understand and suspect that the idea that you could be forgiven for doing really shitty things after you did them, made it that much easier to do said shitty things.

I was twenty-five before the question of how to teach ethics and morality would apply to my own child. Before then, I hadn't really thought about how I was taught right from wrong, or how I would pass that on to my child. I had been taught that the only way to impart those values in a child was through church, but I knew that I didn't want my kid growing up with the idea of divine absolution.

Stripper Mom

By the time my husband and I decided it was time to share our genetics with the world, I had been used to being judged. One of my motivations for going to culinary school was to be able to have a respectable job for when I was a mom. That didn't work out quite as planned. I had quit dancing and was working in a supermarket bakery when I learned I was pregnant. I had been there three days when I couldn't figure out why I was both nauseated and close to hysterical most of the time. I left early on the third, and what would be the final day I was there and picked up a pregnancy test on the way home. Even though I had stopped taking my birth control almost two months prior, I was still shocked to see the double lines on the pee stick.

I had been told it might take a while to get pregnant because I had been on the pill for so long, but that turned out not to be the case. My husband and I were thrilled. Well, him maybe a little more than me. I was terrified. The gravity of being responsible for raising a well-adjusted human being was overwhelming. Being married was all fun and games until you added another life to it. While I had considered all these things before I stopped my birth control pills, it didn't really hit home until I actually became pregnant. I was growing what would be a little person inside me and their life would depend on me. Mind blowing.

I quit my bakery job. I like to blame being around food making my morning sickness worse, but that is simply a cop out on my part. I just hated the job. I got a job with a temp agency and went to work as an administrative assistant. Because the job was only to last for about seven months, it was perfect. I figured I could go back to a bakery after the baby was born. That also didn't go as planned. At around five months, when I felt the fetus kick, I couldn't picture myself handing my two- or three-month old baby to a babysitter. That was when I decided that I would be a stripper mom.

If it wasn't for the fact that I was happily married, I would've been a walking cliché - the old joke about going to a strip club to support single moms. I had already been the stripper working her way through school. So why not be a stripper mom? My husband was making pretty good money, but any job I got after I had the baby would be barely enough to pay for daycare. It just didn't make sense to spend all day working to pay for someone else to raise my kid. I was afraid I would be judged even more harshly though, as a stripper mom, and I wasn't wrong.

The day after our son was born, I got a very unpleasant visitor at the hospital. Someone had alerted Child Protective Services that a druggy stripper had just given birth. Unbeknownst to me, I was already pregnant at my husband's thirtieth birthday. Not knowing I was pregnant, I drank quite a lot of whiskey and smoked pot at his party. Unfortunately, I informed the doctor of this when confirming my home pregnancy test. I had only been off my pill a couple of weeks and didn't think there was any way I could've been pregnant during the party. However, the doctor told me that I had nothing to worry about. From that moment on, I diligently followed the advice in the book *What to Expect When You're Expecting*. I didn't drink, smoke, drink tap water, eat hot dogs, or microwave anything in plastic for the rest of my pregnancy. I had been taking prenatal vitamins for six months before I even stopped taking my birth control. So, when the vile woman in the ugly shoes came in and told me that I was a no good druggy stripper, I was slightly taken aback.

I was immediately defensive. She informed me that, because of my job, I was considered at high risk for reusing marijuana, and that she would need a drug test, which to her obvious disappointment, I passed. When she finally failed at finding any good reason to continue her persecution, she reluctantly left. Case closed. I never heard from her or Child Protective Services again. I still have no idea how she even knew that I had been a stripper to begin with. I never told my doctor. I only told him I had smoked pot before I knew I was pregnant. I certainly didn't tell anyone that I planned to return to stripping when I got back in shape. My guess is that they may have seen it on my tax return. Whatever the case, this whole incident didn't give me a whole lot of confidence as a new mother.

If they thought I was a bad mom because I was a stripper, imagine what people would think if they had known I didn't believe in God? Stripper atheist mom. I figured it would be best to keep the atheist thing to myself, lest someone think I might be planning to sacrifice my child to Satan. If the stereotypes for strippers were already bad, the stereotypes for atheists were even worse. Even strippers thought atheists were bad people. I wasn't sure at all how I was going to handle this whole motherhood thing in the first place. Until I looked at my little poop and barf factory.

Once we got him home, my husband and I would simply stare with awe into the crib. Marveling at our little baby burrito, totally caught off guard by my unexpectedly high tolerance for throw up. If you had asked me how I would react if someone were to pee on me, I would have told you that I would punch them in the face. However, when my son did it, I simply giggled, rolled my eyes, and cleaned it up. The love my husband and I felt for our crotch fruit was overwhelming. Each new milestone was a reason to celebrate. The first poop in the potty caused all three of us to dance.

Being parents made both of us better people. It was just that simple. God or no god, stripper or not, we knew without a doubt that this was the single most important purpose we had. Raising our kid dominated our lives. Everything revolved around him. Without my job, I couldn't have been half the mom I have been because of the time it's given me with him. I've made plenty of mistakes. I've tried to learn from them, and while I try to not repeat past mistakes, I still make them. I am not perfect, and neither is my husband, but we are in it together doing the best we can. It's been fourteen years. I think we have done pretty well. I suppose there is still time for it to go south, but it seems that we are raising a pretty decent human being.

Godless Role Models

As a kid, I learned that humans were all born bad. Dirty rotten sinners right out of the womb, thanks to Eve. Getting baptized would wash away that sin, but God would be watching to make sure you didn't fuck it all up, although he knew you would. Humans, it seemed, just couldn't help that they would want to sin all the time, but God would forgive. God always watching was a common thing for me to hear when I was a kid. It kind of freaked me out. It didn't freak me out enough to stop me from stealing candy, though. Why would it? I knew he was watching and it didn't change my mind because I knew I just had to confess to be forgiven. No worries, just do the bad thing and be forgiven. After all, we were born to be bad, anyway. The problem was that even after accepting the consequences, I didn't forgive myself. I felt like crap. I let down my family, who had taught me better. God wasn't a deterrent at all. My conscience and letting down my family was.

God didn't teach me anything at all about being good. My family did that. I watched my sister raise abandoned baby rabbits, and cry when she lost one. I saw my mom take in stray teenagers and nurture them as her own. My brothers read to me, taught me to swim and kissed my boo boos, and taught me why it was bad to steal. While the church was busy telling me how rotten I was, my family was showing me how to love and be kind. The role models I had in my life were those who taught me to be a good person. The stories I learned from the bible, however, taught me that God was cruel and full of judgement. He was the ultimate hypocrite. He was jealous and mean, and yet demanded to be loved. God was a terrible role model, yet he got all the credit.

188

When we were told that it was fine to not be religious parents but that we should at least have our son baptized, we refused. Baptism is the acknowledgement that our son was born bad and needed to be cleansed. While he required regular baths, I refuse to even superficially entertain the idea that he was born bad. In fact, I think the entire concept of original sin could itself be considered abusive. The message it sends is one of guilt and shame.

Starting out your life with the idea that you are already broken and tainted sets one up to feel bad about themselves. It sets a child up for the idea that they need redemption, which the church has so generously offered. It tells a child not to listen to the voice in their heads that says, "This doesn't feel right," but to try to conform to a hypocritical and confusing set of rules. Rules that are told to them by the very people they depend on for their safety and growth. A child is prepared to believe what the adults in their lives tell them about the world that they are too young to find out on their own. When those adults tell them that they are born with sin, and that information is coming from a magic guy in the sky, they are going to believe them. When that magic guy is used as justification for any acts that may not be in the child's best interest, the child will also be inclined to believe them.

The idea of using God as simply a motivator, or explanation for the unexplainable, may not seem harmful at first. Yet, even this simple concept sets up a child for magical thinking later in life. The child may end up having trouble discerning truth from fiction. They may choose to rely on this type of comfort instead of relying on themselves. That sets them up for disappointment when things they felt were planned for them don't come to fruition. In my opinion, teaching children that they themselves decide what is right, and what they want for life, is a healthier way to go. Let them understand that no one or thing has any power over them other than the power they choose to give away.

I have read a few different articles and studies on the subject of kids raised religious versus kids raised secular. One study, in particular, states that kids raised without religion tend to show more empathy, and also tend to share more. I have also read studies that say kids raised with some sort of faith have a better sense of community and family. Basically, there are studies to back up either position. However, when looking at how the studies were conducted, most of them were based on self-reporting and interviews. Unfortunately, they are simply not conclusive in a scientific way. The one thing I did learn was that the kids who had the best outcomes as the most kind, successful, and happy, all had several things in common, whether religious or secular.

They were all raised in homes where they felt loved, safe, and in homes where empathy and compassion were modeled regularly. The Beatles were right, all you need is love. Well, and a supportive environment where a child feels important, safe, and has someone to look up to. I had thought I looked up to God and Jesus. They were presented as role models, but they only obscured the truth. My role models were my family. They were the people who kept me safe, taught me right from wrong, and showed me how to be kind to other people, as well as to animals. They taught me these things both through their actions and their words. All the while putting the credit where it didn't belong.

Some may see a stripper as an unlikely role model, and I don't have much to say about that. I would be a liar if I said I would be totally thrilled if my son wanted to dance naked for a living. I tell him I will be supportive of whatever path he chooses in life, as long as he does right by other people and by himself. If that means that he chooses to dance naked, well, I would support that, as well. Thankfully, I doubt that will be the case. While I was a stripper, that is not all I am today, and it's not what I set out to model for my kid.

As my own role models did, I try to model kindness and honesty. I try to model helping people where I can, as well as healthy emotional boundaries. My husband and I try to show how a marriage works as a partnership, and our family works as a team. That we are all here to support each other, even if we all do things that kind of suck sometimes. That mistakes are opportunities to learn and grow. We try to emphasize that he has the power to choose his own life, that he is in charge of his own definition of who he is. That he should not be bound to labels that others want to push on him. He is in charge of his own destiny and who he wants to be.

Through all of our parenting exploits, we have never needed to use any supernatural reasoning to explain life. Our son is encouraged to investigate the origins of life and the universe for himself. We want him to come to whatever conclusions are right for him. We don't tell him he should be an atheist. We tell him to look for answers, and we teach him to use reason and logic. We have never had to threaten him with hell - no dessert maybe, but not hell. We have never seen a reason to tell him that he has any reason to be ashamed for simply being alive. We have simply not seen any good reason to involve religion or the concept of god or higher power in our parenting.

We may not look like Ozzie and Harriet, or the Cleavers, but we incorporate all those values in our everyday lives. We have inappropriate dinner conversations, but the fact that we have conversations is the point. We stress that love, empathy, humor, and compassion are the most important things in life. We teach him not that he needs to worry about forgiveness from God if he does something wrong, but from himself or the person he may have wronged. You don't need a god to tell you right from wrong. You know when you've done something wrong. If kids are taught to care about other living creatures, other humans, animals, and even plants, except geraniums, those suck, God serves no purpose. They will know. They will understand how it feels to do good and how it feels to do bad.

I was terrified to be a mom. Afraid that I would fuck it up, and though I still have time to do just that, I think we're on the right track. Regardless of what other people may think about my job or my lack of faith, my son displays genuine empathy. And while his empathy and good nature are sometimes hard to make out through the smart-ass mouth he very much inherited from his mother, he is proof that kids don't need God to learn to be good people.

Chapter 22

Some Strippers Need Jesus

How to Make Acceptance and Boundaries Work Together

It's a quarter to three in the morning, fifteen minutes until closing. The waitress has started wiping down tables and collecting the little electric candles. Hope is waning. It's been a bad night, and by bad I don't mean just slow but really bad. If I didn't know better, I might think that the club put out an advertisement offering discounts to every disrespectful cheap douchebag they could find. I seemed to have attracted every guy with a nearly lethal halitosis condition within a twenty-mile radius, and still found myself irritated that he wouldn't buy a lap dance from me. It seems almost as if I am every other girl's good luck charm tonight because every time someone turns me down, they accept a dance from the next girl who asks. The night is almost over. I am tempted to give up and go home with my measly earnings. For the hours I've worked, I haven't even managed to make minimum wage.

I glance at the entrance, and there he is, my knight in shining cotton. My savior, my last chance at salvaging a miserable night. Most, if not all, the girls are in the VIP or already getting ready to go home. There are no cover charges or stage performances this late at night. The only reason someone would come in so late is to buy lap dances. As the only girl on the floor, his options are limited, and I couldn't be more grateful. Already topless, I approach, and have to say almost nothing before he swiftly walks with me back to the VIP. He asks how my night has gone, and against my better judgement I confess that it has been extraordinarily shitty. I usually don't complain to customers, on the assumption that they are here for a good time, not to be burdened with my problems. But, every once in a while, I tell the truth, despite it being blatantly unprofessional. Every once in a while, it works to my advantage.

He says, "You're so beautiful, I don't believe you could ever have a bad night." I am very fond of this guy all of a sudden. He proceeds to tell me, as I delicately grind in his lap, how stupid and blind the assholes are to whom I have been subjected all night. He buys all the songs the DJ will play before turning on all the lights and informing everybody, which consists of just me and my new favorite customer, that we don't have to go home but we can't stay here. He gives me a hug and tips me generously before leaving the club, never to be seen again.

I was so close to giving up, the only reason I was on the floor and not in the dressing room getting ready to leave, dejected and broke, was the small, tiny remnant of hope that I might be able to get a late customer. It wasn't something that happened often. It required patience and diligence which can be hard to muster after a bad night. I believed that I might be able to pull it off, but only if I didn't give up. If I had held a belief in some sort of higher power, I might have gone so far as to consider this a miracle.

Behold! A stripper miracle! I know that as miraculous as it seemed, to have spent all night being rejected, feeling about as attractive as a damp gym sock, only to be saved by a slightly inebriated man at the last possible second, wasn't a miracle. At least, not in the supernatural sense. No unseen force had my back. It wasn't karma, or an answered prayer. The reason this worked out for me was because I refused to give up. That I would not admit defeat until I was absolutely sure I had done everything I could to change my night. I took pride in the fact that I didn't give up and was ultimately rewarded for my efforts. Of course, when I relayed my good fortune with the only other stripper still in the dressing room, she said, "Someone must have been looking out for you".

Without saying it, I know that she meant that God, the universe, Jesus, or some force other than beer and loneliness caused the guy who happened to like redheads to come in and buy dances from me. To be totally fair, he might not have even been into redheads. After all, he didn't really have any other options, but let's just pretend he was. The idea that blind luck and my own fortitude were the real reasons this happened wasn't something this other stripper even considered. Whatever her thoughts, she felt like she needed to believe something was looking out for me in my time of need and was happy for me. For her, it gave her hope that when it came time for her to have a bad night, someone might be looking out for her, too.

Something to Believe In

Because the original motivating factor behind my writing was to dispel the image that all strippers are broken and damaged, I don't write a lot about the fact that there are some strippers who come from very rough childhoods and backgrounds. My thought being that this was a story that has already been told. The story of the abused girl who now felt like her only option was to strip. The stripper who got into drugs and started dancing to pay for her habit. The stripper who put up with abuse from her boyfriend. Dr. Phil has covered all that. I wanted to tell the story of a stripper who liked performing naked. The stripper who found nudity empowering and liberating. I wanted to tell the story of the stripper with a happy ending. While I feel like I did that, I can't ignore the fact that there are strippers who fit the more dire stereotypes.

Throughout my career, I have heard many disturbing stories of abuse, neglect, and addiction. Some of these stories are before or after a girl has started dancing. There are girls who enter sex work because they think it's their only option. There are girls who entered stripping because they wanted to, but ended up falling into one trap or another, keeping them there. Drugs, alcohol, and bad relationships are the kind of traps that can sneak up on someone. Especially if they are young and naive. You may walk into a strip club as a girl full of wonder and excitement, just to leave feeling rejected and hopeless. It happens. Sometimes these girls have no one to turn to, and do not have the strength to empower themselves to change.

I have made my objections clear when it comes to the outreach group that comes in to save strippers. These Christians push the narrative that stripping was a mistake God wanted you to make. I feel that is fucked up in a lot of ways. The talk of a divine plan that includes abuse and drugs is abhorrent to me because it leaves no room for personal responsibility. It justifies bad behavior and poor choices and implies that the only way to get out is through Jesus. The belief system it is founded on is deeply flawed when examined closely. It simply replaces a situation where someone already feels worthless with an ideology that asserts they are indeed worthless, from birth. However, if taken superficially, without applying logic and reason, in some cases it can be helpful.

Wait, what? When in a place of utter despair, and I have seen girls in just such a place, any offer of hope or support is worth considering. If someone needs the idea of Jesus to help them start to make better choices, then who am I to tell them no? I don't think it is the best route, by any stretch of the imagination, but if it saves someone from overdosing, or gives them access to resources to get them away from an abusive partner, then I am all for it. Logic and reason be damned. Some strippers may just need Jesus.

Not everyone can handle the thought that they are on their own. If a girl or woman is in such a state that they feel hopeless, I think where that hope comes from is moot. At least in the moment. Many women in the sex industry can harbor feelings of abandonment. To work through those feelings, they may need to think there is a force working for them behind the scenes. Honestly, in dangerous and potentially lethal situations, I don't care what helps women out of it. Logic and reason can come later, or not. If someone has used magical thinking, like the idea of a higher power, for most of their lives, pulling the rug out from under them seems kind of cruel if they are in a bad way.

Personally, I never found comfort in any type of religion or deity. I was simply unable to convince myself that they were based in any sort of reality. Not that I didn't try. I prayed and tried to find comfort in those things. The problem was the little voice in my head that refused to go along with it. I had a stubborn, little reason demon in the back of my mind always saying, "Really? You sure?" No matter what I did, he was always there pointing out the mundane and very un-supernatural reason for something that happened or didn't happen. That little bugger was constantly debunking any sort of miracle or divine cause for the things in my life. When I finally stopped ignoring him, things got much better and less confusing for me. I reveled in my own empowerment. Accepting that I alone am responsible for my life and choices was one of the best things I have done for myself. I was able to be comfortable once and for all with not knowing stuff. Not everything required an answer, and that was totally OK. In fact, not knowing can be the fun part of life because it leaves room for learning and wonder. I found that I am much happier accepting that not everything has an answer than trying to believe there is a God to fill those knowledge gaps.

That type of thinking is not easy for many people. I have been through some shit for sure, but my experiences pale in comparison to some of the women I have met. Assuming they will be able to find the same kind of comfort as I have is simply unfair. It is not reasonable to believe that everyone copes in the same way. That is not to imply that they are cognitively challenged or less intelligent, but our thinking and coping skills develop over time and through experience. I think there are some people who may never be able to let go of the concepts they were raised with. In other words, atheism is not for everyone. Not everyone is blessed with a reason demon.

I have been on the receiving end of much criticism not only for being a stripper but also for being an atheist. I do think it is important to accept other people's belief systems, though, no matter how goofy. There are some caveats to acceptance, however. When deeply held beliefs are questioned, the cognitive dissonance can be strong. The need to defend and convince other people of your own beliefs, especially when they rely solely on faith, which by definition is the belief without evidence, is strong. Believers on the defense can become both verbally and physically threatening. Mostly, the threats are in the form of punishment after death, but still, hearing, "You'll be sorry," can be pretty unnerving, not to mention irritating. Unless everyone starts taking John Lennon's words to heart and imagines a world without religion, we will likely all have to be able to make peace with the believers in our lives.

Jesus Boundaries

As a stripper, one of the main reasons I have been successful is my ability to create and maintain personal boundaries. Something I wish strip club Jesus would learn to do. Underwear should simply be a fundamental boundary, at least in terms of a lap dance.

Boundaries in my opinion are the single most important thing in any personal relationship. Whether it is a business or romantic partner, family or friend, strip club patron or staff, boundaries are what keep us emotionally, and sometimes even physically, safe. Establishing where your red lines or deal breakers are will protect your own well-being. When it comes to family, friends, and people you really care about, this can be difficult. Yet, if you really love and care about someone and they feel the same, then establishing boundaries that work for both of you will help preserve the relationship.

Because I find most religious beliefs kind of, forgive me for being mean, stupid, I have been hostile to religious people when I should not have been. Shortly after we purchased our house, our neighbors came to visit. An older lady had introduced herself to my husband. He invited her into our back yard to meet me. I was taking a swim in our pool and was in a bikini. The lady who I will call Ethel, insisted on giving me a hug even though I was wet, which resulted in boob shaped wet spots on her shirt. She laughed, and I thought she could just be the nicest person I had ever met, until I met Fred, her husband. Fred was also incredibly nice. We couldn't have been more pleased with our new neighbors. Then we saw their license plate frames, which clearly advertised a Mormon college. It turns out they were super, I mean really, REALLY Mormon.

No biggie, it's not like they even told us they were Mormon. It was just something they were. They were still wonderful neighbors to have. On the night when there was a lunar eclipse, Fred had his telescope out and asked my son if he wanted to look, which he did. A few days later, Fred brought over a professionally printed glossy photograph to give to our son. Even knowing that at one point Mormons believed and acted on the belief that black people were cursed from God, and something about magic underwear, Fred and Ethel proved through their own actions that they were good people. If they're hiding dismembered bodies or something in their freezer, I would never be able to tell simply judging from our interactions.

Christmas came and went. We exchanged cookies and greetings. Fred and Ethel kept an eye on our house when we went out of town, and never failed to smile and say something nice. We really couldn't have asked for better neighbors, weird religion or not. Then one day, Ethel knocked on my door with a pie in her hand. She told me that her church group had extra chicken pot pies and she thought we might like one to save me a night of cooking. So naturally, I told her I didn't accept anything from the church. She simply took the pie back to her house, leaving me feeling immediately like an asshole.

I thought about what I had said and why. Why did it bother me so much that a Mormon lady had made a pie and offered it to me? It wasn't like they had been assholes or anything, ever. She wasn't condescending in offering it to me, quite the opposite, in fact. I had cooking discussions with Ethel before and she knew that I cooked six nights a week. She was really being considerate and genuine in her offer. There was no real objection to the pie that I could think of except that I simply didn't like her religion. Neither Fred nor Ethel had ever brought up religion in any conversation at all, not even at Christmas. Never had they mentioned their faith at all. I had been in their living room, noticed all the Mormon books, and that was how I knew. They were even considerate enough to move their cars every year to accommodate parking for our annual 4th of July party. Which can get pretty boisterous. No, there was no legitimate reason for me to have been an ass.

I walked down and knocked on Fred and Ethel's door. Ethel answered. I began to stammer an apology. For the record, I dislike apologizing, especially when I've been an asshole. It took me a few tries to get this right. I told Ethel I appreciated her offer, had judged too quickly, and wrongly assumed that somehow the pot pie represented an offer to be a part of the church. With much more grace than I had, she told me she understood, adding that it was simply a gesture of kindness. We exchanged a few more pleasantries and I went back to my home with a freshly made chicken pot pie. Which by the way, turned out to be delicious, almost worth sitting through a Mormon bible study. Just kidding, nothing would be that delicious.

I would never have thought that a chicken pot pie would hold such an important lesson in acceptance. I have spent so much of my life and career looking for other people to accept me and also looking to accept myself, that I lost sight of the need to accept other people. I don't need to accept Mormonism or any other ism I don't agree with in order to accept the person behind it. I have complained so many times about people who don't want to look past my job or my own lack of faith, but sometimes failed to do the same. Especially in terms of religion.

I had become very proficient creating boundaries in the strip club, but this pie incident made me consider my boundaries concerning other parts of my life. How many people have I alienated simply for their faith? What and where are my boundaries in terms of religious belief? If someone says they will pray for me, do I tell them to fuck off? Don't bother wishing for me? That would be shitty. I simply say thank you and recognize that they are trying to be nice. That's it. If someone mentions their faith in conversation, should I interrupt and tell them their beliefs are stupid? That would also be shitty. I have decided that whatever someone's belief, anything from faith in alternative medicine to religion, if they aren't trying to push me to believe what they do, we can be cool. If someone finds comfort in crystals or burning sage to rid their house of negative energy, if they aren't trying to tell me to do so, then that's just fine.

If someone takes comfort in going to church, fine. I can't deny that there is often a sense of community in churches that people find worth having in their lives. I might counter that: You can find that same sense of community with atheist groups, as well, but it doesn't matter. Bottom line, if someone's beliefs are benign and cause no harm to themselves or others, I have no issue. I once had a long conversation with a devout Christian. When we got down to it, we both had the same morals. The morals just came from vastly different places. I think most religious people tend to deliberately overlook the origins and fundamental ideas of their respective holy books. They simply don't want to know. Just ask a Christian if Jesus had been executed by guillotine, if they would be comfortable wearing a tiny guillotine hung on a gold chain around their necks. Probably not. A noose or a machete wouldn't look so hot, either. It's willful ignorance, and it's annoying, but if it's not harmful, it's not my business.

So, when is it appropriate to cut someone off for their beliefs? Simply put, when they are abusive. When they are so toxic that it is affecting your own happiness. I wish I could give you a distinct list of criteria, but I can't. Every person and relationship is different. People who love you and are truly afraid that you will go to hell may believe they are well intended. They may actually be worried for you. But, if they are unwilling to accept your boundaries, you may have to put some distance in the relationship. Each relationship must be individually evaluated. If someone you care about is a constant source of stress, then you may have to let them go. I have had to do this, and it super sucks, but was necessary to preserve my own values and happiness.

When it comes to other supernatural ideas and pseudoscience, I have to resist the urge to debunk everything someone says, but I still do sometimes. I recently explained the phenomenon of sleep paralysis in the context of ghosts and apparitions, as I've mentioned in this book, and that person is now mad at me. They really didn't want that information, and I offered it uninvited. My information was sort of like a ghost that holds you down to scream in your face. When I thought about it, their belief in ghosts wasn't causing any harm, but I had just finished reading about it and felt the need to share. I should have kept my mouth shut though, because all I did was upset them. They still believe in ghosts. They also now believe that I am an asshole. Not sure I can debunk that one entirely.

Ultimately, I think it comes down to harm. If someone wants to believe in God, and that doesn't cause harm to anyone else, let them have it. If someone wants to believe that finding a penny is good luck, why the hell not? If someone, however, thinks they can heal cancer with prayer and prayer alone, well, then, maybe it's time to have a little chat about going to the doctor as a supplement to prayer. You know, just in case there's a glitch in the line to heaven.

Sometimes, people simply want or need to have their beliefs to cope, and atheists can seem to be just as aggressive as theists. I think it is just as inappropriate to try to get someone to stop believing in God as it is to knock on someone's door to tell them they are going to hell. Relationships are about communication and respect, and sometimes that simply means keeping your fucking mouth shut. Accepting the people we choose to have in our lives can enrich the time we have on earth. Finding appropriate boundaries can help us make sure we are making the most of the time we have with the people we love.

Chapter 23

Expose Yourself

When You Take Risks, You Find Yourself

When I first became a stripper, I thought I was simply exposing my naked body, but it went much further than that. I wasn't happy with my life to the extent that I was willing to risk quite a lot by entering a profession I really didn't know much about except that it wasn't something respectable women did. I simply knew I didn't like the future that was stretching out in front of me. I knew so many people who were pretending to be happy, living what most people considered a normal life. I felt I was supposed to do what people wanted or told me to do. I thought I should do what people said would make me happy or a productive member of society. Whatever that means. What I did instead was to take a risk.

A risk at not being normal. I refused to sink quietly into that office chair of regret, resentment, and bitterness. I took a risk to be happy. I finally decided, what the hell? What do I have to lose? It turned out, I had plenty to lose. I lost my sense of confinement and conformity. I lost my sense of being part of the crowd. I lost the feeling of dread that came from going to a job I hated. I lost my poor self-confidence. I lost the part of me that felt like I had to please everybody. I lost my chance to be just like everyone else. I actually lost quite a lot by becoming a stripper. But I found some things too.

I found my independence. I found my love of performing. I found that taking risks meant learning. I found the courage to stop pretending to believe in things I knew were false. I also found the courage to seek answers to questions I was told not to ask. I found comfort in the answers I found, while I also learned to be comfortable with questions that had no answers. I found wonder in

203

things science hasn't answered yet, and the excitement of trying to find out. I found the joy of exploring a world beyond the confines of belief. I found that simply not knowing was much better for me than trying to accept answers that were made up. I found myself.

When we expose ourselves to the world, we remove the shelter we may have had from judgement and criticism. The protection that comes from keeping certain parts of us hidden can be comforting but ultimately limits the possibilities for living our best lives. How strong are the connections we make to other people if we are hiding who we really are? How do you live a life without regrets if you deny what makes you unique? We are taught to believe we are all as individual as snowflakes, and yet we are still encouraged to be like everyone else. Take the safe route, be what society tells you to be or your life will suck. Don't take that risk or you will be sorry, maybe even forever.

Exposing ourselves can leave us feeling vulnerable, maybe even isolated. The good news is, as unique as you are, currently there are something like 7.7 billion people in the world. Statistically speaking, that leaves a lot of chances to find people who are quite a lot like you. People who will understand and relate to your individual experiences. When I gave up pretending to believe in God, I thought I was going to be left standing alone. That was not even close to the case. I found so many people who thought like me, and were more than willing to accept me as I am. With so many people in the world, you don't ever have to feel alone. Sometimes leaving the shelter of conformity exposes you to a community you may not have known existed. Stripping taught me that however unconventional, I could find acceptance. I rejected the plan other people told me I should have. I also found the confidence to reject beliefs I was told to hold. I found the courage to make my own plan. I stopped waiting for someone to show me my path or purpose. I think the funniest thing is that I ended up wanting a fairly normal life, after all. I love taking care of my house and my family. I love doing all the normal things I thought I was rejecting. The difference was that it was now my choice. When I put on my apron to bake for the afternoon, I look like a scene out of a Norman Rockwell painting, if only because you can't hear the death metal in the background. Except for the whole stripping thing, it turns out the life I really wanted was pretty normal, after all.

Once I exposed who I wanted to be, and what I wanted out of life, I started to expose myself to knowledge about the world. When I mentioned to someone I was reading a book by the astrophysicist Carl Sagan, I was told to be careful. That was a slippery slope. Hell, yes it was. I wondered what his comment meant. That seemed like such a weird thing to say, but I realized he was right. I slipped right into books by physicists, sociologists, biologists, and other freethinkers. I had no idea how much I had to learn. I didn't realize how many people aren't bound by belief. How many people actually rejected the idea that there were things we just weren't meant to know. The fact is, there are many things we don't understand yet, but that doesn't mean we aren't capable. One of the most wonderful things I have come to learn is how many people out there are asking questions and looking for answers. People who plainly reject the idea that we simply can't know. We can know those things, we just don't yet.

When we look for the truth in our lives it exposes the deceptions that are presented to us. When you look for the truth, unwilling to accept answers without evidence, you rebuild the shelter that you may have lost when you exposed yourself to the world. You are able to spot the bullshit that masquerades as fact. When you learn to question everything, you expose those who take advantage of innocent ignorance. Pseudoscience, conspiracies, and the superstitions that haunt our world are no longer a threat to you. Those who want to scare you into believing things that aren't true, to further whatever agenda they may have, are easier to spot. You are able to evaluate what risks are worth taking and what risks are not. You no longer have to be afraid of the things you don't understand. When you expose yourself to the truth that we can know, you are protecting yourself from the harm that comes from a shelter built out of bullshit.

Bibliography

I unexpectedly learned a lot about life and people from stripping, but most of my practical knowledge comes from my love of books and reading. While stripping has the potential to teach you much about the world and the people in it, it is obviously not for everyone. At the risk of sounding like I'm plugging certain books, I would like to share some of the books and authors I have read that I found interesting and enlightening. My intention is not to advertise, as there are probably thousands of great books that will help further your knowledge on a range of subjects. Just to put a fine point on it, I have no vested interest in any of these books or authors, whatsoever.

I consider books to be doors in an endless hallway of information, knowledge, and wonder. Each door leads to another path of information. This list is simply meant to show you a few of those doors. Whether you choose to open any of them is entirely up to you. Even fiction is full of insight, enlightenment, and a chance to experience a different perspective. While I love non-fiction, fiction is still my favorite. Fiction is its own door, but one that provides a peek into someone else's imagination. Fictional characters can shine a light on our innermost thoughts and inspire an examination of our own desires. However you choose to live your life, never stop learning. Take it from a stripper, exposing yourself to new knowledge is always worth the risk.

Rewire Your Anxious Brain: How to Use the Neuroscience of Fear to End Anxiety, Panic and Worry ~ by Catherine M Pittman and Elizabeth M Karle, MLIS

I know, a stripper with anxiety, how droll. But I have struggled with anxiety for a large part of my life. This book helped me understand why the little anxiety hamster that lives in my brain simply refused to stop running in loops on its wheel. It also helped me stop that little bugger. Neuroscience is a branch of science that uses a mixture of physiology, anatomy, molecular and developmental biology, cytology, mathematical modeling and psychology to help understand neurons and neural circuits in the brain. One hell of a mouthful, I know, but this book is written in an easy way for the layperson to understand. It has many useful techniques to understand the causes and remedies for anxiety. This book is also helpful in teaching you what things are actually risky, and what things simply make you nervous but aren't really dangerous.

Spook ~ by Mary Roach

This lady is a science writer and a humorous one at that. Shortly after I lost my nephew, I started to research the afterlife. This was my first read. She investigates all manner of claims about the afterlife. From mediums to a 1901 experiment by a physician on tuberculosis patients, who weighed terminal patients at the exact time of death to see if their souls could be measured. Add in stories of reincarnation and near-death experiences, she really leaves no stone unturned. She keeps it entertaining the whole way. It is a lighthearted read with a lot of great information, probably one of my favorite non-fiction books of all time.

God No! ~ by Penn Jillette

My first book on atheism. Of Penn and Teller, Penn is the loud one. Just in case you aren't familiar with Penn, listen to the audio version of this book and you'll hear exactly what I mean, as he narrates it himself. I'm not going to sugar coat it, this book is a little harsh. Penn is blunt about his opinions and very matter of fact. Frankly, if you can handle my book, you can probably handle his, but I wouldn't recommend it to your grandma.

Unpersuadables: Adventures with the Enemies of Science ~ by Will Storr

I recommend this book to anyone who wants to understand how people can believe utter bullshit. How is it people are able to suspend common sense and defy logic in order to believe all sorts of abject nonsense? This book explores, using neuroscience and psychology, how people can give in to self-deception. This was helpful for me to understand why some people simply couldn't let go of deeply held beliefs, and actually helped me find some compassion and acceptance toward them. Although my previous disclaimer about harm to self or others still applies, the path to acceptance of other people comes from understanding them.

A Brief History of Time ~ by Stephen Hawking

A stripper reading about physics, surely you must be joking. I'm not and don't call me Shirley. A strong cup of coffee was required for this one, not because it was boring but because it called for fierce focus. It goes without saying that Stephen Hawking was a smart guy. He was a great writer as well. Physics (and math if I'm being honest), was a subject I mostly blew off in school, but as I accepted my atheism, I ran across some concepts that I just didn't understand. This book helped me gain a basic layman's grasp on the subject of astrophysics.

God is Not Great: How Religion Poisons Everything ~ by Christopher Hitchens

From start to finish, Christopher Hitchens dismantles religion at every turn. He's a bit of a smart-ass, so I loved him from the very beginning. Unfortunately, I found out after I read this book that he had passed away from cancer. I can't tell you what a loss that has been for the atheist community he left behind. You can see many of his debates with theists online. He is a master at using reason and logic to clap back at some of the ridiculous moral arguments people use to justify religion. This book in particular illustrates the harm that organized religion has caused throughout the world.

The God Delusion ~ by Richard Dawkins

Probably one of the most read books on atheism. Richard Dawkins is an evolutionary biologist, and from what I can tell through his writing, is one of the nicest people alive. He very skillfully explains evolution and how it pretty much rules out an intelligent designer. What he also does is explain altruism in almost all species. I would recommend any of his writings, but for those just beginning to explore atheism, this is a great start. He has some humorous points, but never mean spirited, ever.

Sex and God: How Religion Distorts Sexuality ~ by Darrel Ray

I thought I had learned everything about this subject from my job. I was so wrong. This book explained the reasons behind some of the depravity I have encountered as a stripper. It is also hilarious at some points. I listened to the audio version and very nearly face planted on the treadmill as he was explaining duck penises. I'll resist spoiling it for you, but if you are interested in how religion influences sexual biology, this is the book for you. Darrel Ray is also an atheist activist who helped found the organization Recovering from Religion, and the Secular Therapy Project. These types of organizations help people deal with the trauma and ostracization that can come from leaving a religious sect.

The Demon-Haunted World: Science as a Candle in the Dark ~ by Carl Sagan and Ann Druyan

When I read this book, I was most disturbed by its prophetic descriptions of what happens when misinformation makes it into the mainstream. I very nearly forgot that it was written in 1995. It explains the scientific method beautifully. Ironically, he debunks psychics' ability to predict the future, while seemingly predicting the future of pseudoscience and the manipulation of technology to spread myths. It is a wonderful read and was indeed a slippery slope to many more books on science.

The Skeptics' Guide to the Universe: How to Know What's Really Real in a World Increasingly Full of Fake ~ by Stephen Novella, Bob Novella, and Cara Santa Maria

We are bombarded by fake information everywhere we look. This book lays out exactly how to identify and debunk bullshit. It will not make you fun at parties, however. This book gave me the tools to piss off just about everyone I know. And they don't even tackle the god question. From chiropractors, to flat earthers, to anti-vaxxers, to ghosts, they point out just how much fake is out there and how to get around it. This is, in my opinion, one of the most important books to read today. It can help you see not only your own cognitive biases, but recognize the biases in other people. The authors also have ongoing podcasts and blogs to combat every new piece of bullshit that emerges today, mostly emerging on the internet. As you can imagine, they keep very busy.

Boobliography

Books by Yours Truly

Dirty Money: Memoirs of a Stripper

My first book. I take you year by year through my life and career. My goal with this book was to explain my choices and why stripping doesn't have to be a bad thing for everyone. Not so much a memoir in the strict definition of the word, more of an autobiography.

Think You Want to be a Stripper?

This book was meant to be a parting gift to future strippers. I offer my opinions and advice on the industry. As well as a gritty behind the scenes look at the profession itself. It is not so much meant to encourage girls to enter the industry, just to inform and entertain. It seems to entertain everyone, not just aspiring strippers. Enjoy.

Freedom From Religion Foundation

www.ffrf.org

The Freedom From Religion Foundation is an advocacy group for the separation of church and state. I learned about them initially online, then much more about their work when I went to their convention. The many dedicated people they have in their ranks work tirelessly to protect our freedom from religion in our government. With most of their work being done in the courts, a lot of what they do is behind the scenes but is extremely important in protecting our democracy.

In addition to the legal work they do, FFRF also provides a network for people who have left their various faiths. In other words, they provide a safe place to land for those who have had the courage to come out as atheist, agnostic, or freethinkers. FFRF led me to a widespread community where critical thinking and Humanist philosophy is valued. If you are a closeted atheist, FFRF is a great place to find resources for help coming out of religion. Won't you please check them out and consider becoming a member?

Contact Ms. Louis

Website	ErinLouis.com
Email	Erin@ErinLouis.com
Facebook	Search for ErinLouis666
Twitter	Search for ErinLouis666
Patreon	Search for Brazen Atheist

Made in the USA
Columbia, SC
06 August 2019